Topz Holiday Club

Mission: Miracle Maker

Emma Smallwood and Jeni Wilson

CWR

NATIONAL DISTRIBUTORS

UK: (and countries not listed below)
CWR, Waverley Abbey House, Waverley Lane, Farnham, Surrey GU9 8EP.
Tel: (01252) 784710 Outside UK (44) 1252 784710

AUSTRALIA: CMC Australasia, PO Box 519, Belmont, Victoria 3216.
Tel: (03) 5241 3288

CANADA: Cook Communications Ministries, PO Box 98, 55 Woodslee Avenue, Paris, Ontario
Tel: 1800 263 2664

GHANA: Challenge Enterprises of Ghana, PO Box 5723, Accra.
Tel: (021) 222437/223249 Fax: (021) 226227

HONG KONG: Cross Communications Ltd, 1/F, 562A Nathan Road, Kowloon.
Tel: 2780 1188 Fax: 2770 6229

INDIA: Crystal Communications, 10-3-18/4/1, East Marredpally, Secunderabad – 500 026.
Tel/Fax: (040) 7732801

KENYA: Keswick Books and Gifts Ltd, PO Box 10242, Nairobi.
Tel: (02) 331692/226047 Fax: (02) 728557

MALAYSIA: Salvation Book Centre (M) Sdn Bhd, 23 Jalan SS 2/64,
47300 Petaling Jaya, Selangor.
Tel: (03) 78766411/78766797 Fax: (03) 78757066/78756360

NEW ZEALAND: CMC Australasia, PO Box 36015, Lower Hutt.
Tel: 0800 449 408 Fax: 0800 449 049

NIGERIA: FBFM, Helen Baugh House, 96 St Finbarr's College Road, Akoka, Lagos.
Tel: (01) 7747429/4700218/825775/827264

PHILIPPINES: OMF Literature Inc, 776 Boni Avenue, Mandaluyong City.
Tel: (02) 531 2183 Fax: (02) 531 1960

REPUBLIC OF IRELAND: Scripture Union, 40 Talbot Street, Dublin 1.
Tel: (01) 8363764

SINGAPORE: Armour Publishing Pte Ltd, Block 203A Henderson Road,
11–06 Henderson Industrial Park, Singapore 159546.
Tel: 6 276 9976 Fax: 6 276 7564

SOUTH AFRICA: Struik Christian Books, 80 MacKenzie Street,
PO Box 1144, Cape Town 8000.
Tel: (021) 462 4360 Fax: (021) 461 3612

SRI LANKA: Christombu Books, 27 Hospital Street, Colombo 1.
Tel: (01) 433142/328909

TANZANIA: CLC Christian Book Centre, PO Box 1384, Mkwepu Street, Dar es Salaam.
Tel/Fax (022) 2119439

USA: Cook Communications Ministries, PO Box 98, 55 Woodslee Avenue, Paris, Ontario, Canada
Tel: 1800 263 2664

ZIMBABWE: Word of Life Books, Shop 4, Memorial Building,
35 S Machel Avenue, Harare.
Tel: (04) 781305 Fax: (04) 774739

For email addresses, visit the CWR website: www.cwr.org.uk

CWR is a registered charity – number 294387

With juggernauts of thanks to our Educate friends, especially David and Var. It's a pleasure to work with you. We pray that God will take us to more exciting work – to infinity and beyond! Thanks for putting up with us even when we're stressy or slightly crazy and for helping us out when time was against us. Thanks too to our friends, Daniel, Alisha, Max and Sophie, whose practical help was crucial. You're stars! Thanks to Caz for all your help arranging and recording the *Mission: Miracle Maker* song. It sounds really good! Thank you, Caroline, for letting us use your recording equipment!

Published 2003 by CWR, Waverley Abbey House, Waverley Lane, Farnham, Surrey GU9 8EP.

Concept development, editing, design and production by CWR.
Illustrator: Helen Reason
Printed in Croatia by Zrinski
ISBN 1-85345-256-4

Contents | Page

Introduction – some things to think about before you begin	2
Getting Started – an easy-to-follow guide	3
Venue – choosing and decorating it	4–5
Promote It! – how and where, so the kids will know about your club	6
Legal Stuff – very important to sort out as you plan your club	6–7
Order, Order! – how to discipline and reward the kids	8
Emergency Smergency! – explanation of the game and emergency procedures	8
Equipment Needed – including checklist	9
Letter to Parent/Guardian – sample letter that can be photocopied or adapted	10
Permission Form – sample form that can be photocopied or adapted	11
The Crew – who you need and how to train them	12–13
Snonge Space Passport Master – ready to be photocopied	14
Mission: Miracle Maker Song Words – ready to be photocopied onto acetate	15
Mission: Miracle Maker Song Music	16–17
Picture of King Snorg – ready to be photocopied onto acetate	18
Day 1 – God becomes human!	19–26
Day 2 – Jesus can even control the fish!	27–35
Day 3 – Jesus heals!	36–44
Day 4 – Jesus raises people from the dead!	45–53
Day 5 – Jesus is still alive!	54–62
Resources available from CPO	inside back cover

The material for each day includes:

- basic timings for the session
- synopsis of the video clip being used
- an aim for the session
- masters of worksheets, Homequests and craft activities
- explanations of games and activities.

Introduction

This material has been designed so that you will have *all* you need to run an activity week, holiday club or short series for a weekly or monthly club, for children between the ages of 5 and 11 (from school year 0 up to and including year 6). We hope that it will be useful for both the experienced children's worker and the first-time leader.

Before you begin planning, you need to think about why you want to run the club. Who you are running it for? What is your vision for the club?

It's an amazing opportunity for a church or Christian organisation to serve a community and make contact with families who otherwise would never step inside a church. Obviously you will want to offer places to children in your church, but it's important to encourage them to invite their friends to come. This is a good way of developing relationships that have already begun.

You also need to think ahead. Would your church/organisation be able to cope with a whole load of new unchurched Christians or children aged 5 to 11 interested in God? What kind of events could you run afterwards to involve families and maintain contact with the children? Could you organise a family service at your church, or a celebration with a group of churches to end the week?

Does the rest of your church feel a part of this outreach? Does it fit in with the vision of your organisation? It's good to get together with leaders of other ministries in your church or other churches in your area to make sure you are working together, and to get prayer support, or extra leaders and resources.

So what will the kids be doing at *Mission: Miracle Maker*? Here's a very basic overview of the week.

When you've done all the necessary preparations and the children are ready to come in, they will be given Snonge Space Passports, which will enable them to enter the *Millennium Parrot* spaceship.

While on board they will be given their mission by King Snorg from the planet Snonge. Each day they will look at a different miracle of Jesus. The morning programme (you can obviously adapt it if you are doing a weekly club or want to do it in the afternoon instead) consists of a mixture of games, music, craft, discussion, video (by the end of the week they will have watched the whole of *The Miracle Maker*) and drama. For some parts of it, the children will be all together, and for others they will split into Starbusters (for 5- to 7-year-olds) and Moonrakers (for 8- to 11-year-olds). (You can also adapt this, depending on what ages you end up with and how your church groups are split.) The craft they make will create a 'view' and go into the five 'windows' of the ship (i.e. be put on the wall!).

Each day the children will be given a Topz Homequest sheet to read and work on if they want to. At the end of the week they will be allowed to bring a visitor (parent/guardian) to visit the ship, hear the song, and take their craftwork home.

Getting Started

First things first – you need to *pray*. We can't do anything without God and, if we want Him to help us and do some amazing things in the lives of the kids, we need to ask Him! Set up a Satellite Prayer Team who will individually pray for the preparation and then pray together as the club is going on or pray specifically for individual children (see page 13). Now get together with a few others and make some decisions. We suggest you start planning about four months before the club starts.

Where are you going to hold the club? (See page 4 for details about the venue.) You can then work out what your maximum number of kids is.

How will you decorate the venue (see page 5)? Maybe you want to set up a small team to be in charge of designing the layout and buying all the materials.

When are you going to have it? Make sure your dates don't clash with anything important.

What ages are you going to offer the club to, and how will you split the two groups?

How much money do you have? Decide on a budget. Maybe you need to get an offering or do some fund-raising.

Do you want events to run after the club for the kids and their families?

How many leaders will you need (see pages 12–13 on the crew)? You will need to organise a date for training. Start asking people to join the crew!

How are you going to promote the club in schools/at church (see page 6)?

Sort out all the legal stuff (see page 6).

Decide on your discipline procedures, which Emergency Smergencies you're going to use and where your fire assembly point outside the building is going to be (see page 8).

Invite the children and sort out registration (see page 11). Send the parents/guardians a letter and permission form (see pages 10 – 11).

Train your leaders – include drama rehearsals (see page 13)!

Make sure you have all you need for each day's activities (see page 9).

Decorate your venue (see page 5).

Keep praying!

Venue

When deciding on your venue you need to take into consideration that legally you will need 25 square feet of floor space per child (this is the requirement for children aged three to eight years). Some other important things to look at ... Your venue needs to be warm, well-ventilated, clean and well-lit. Make sure you've got *insurance cover* for the premises. It should comply with *Health and Safety regulations*, and have adequate *fire doors*, with access to a *telephone* (can be a mobile) and a *first-aid kit*.

So once that's sorted and it's all booked you need to transform your venue into the *Millennium Parrot* spaceship.

Ideally you want:

- The Spaceship – a larger room set up with a stage area
- Passport Control – outside the main doors to the spaceship, for Check-in and Check-out
- Engine Rooms 1 and 2 – two separate rooms/areas for the Starbusters and Moonrakers, set up for the craft activities – preferably straight off the spaceship!
- Satellite Prayer Room for the others to come and pray for the club
- Toilets and hand basins – one of each to ten children
- Refreshments/tuck shop area – you may want to set this up specifically for the break and then take it away again. (NB – if you are going to prepare food on the premises, you need to get them checked out by the Environmental Health Office.)

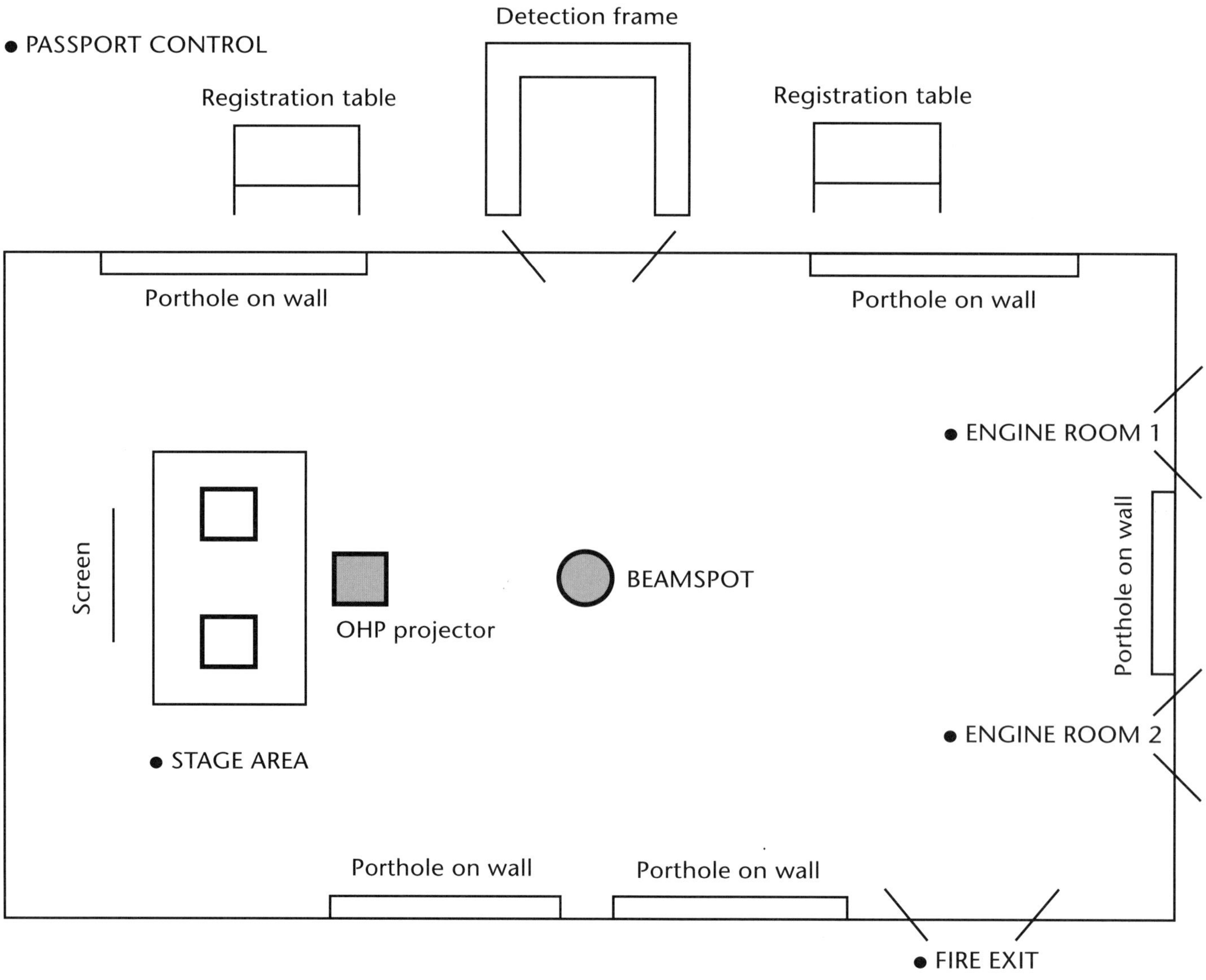

How to Transform Your Venue ... to the Millennium Parrot Spaceship!

Passport Control

Detection frame

This is for the kids to walk through to get onto the spaceship. This can be easily made, using two columns of piled-up cardboard boxes, with an adjoining piece of card over the top. Once all is sprayed silver, or covered in silver foil, you have yourself an authentic Snonge detection frame – nothing will get past it! For a bit more fun, you could cover a torch in red acetate and shine it over the kids as they come in – for extra security reasons, of course!

Check-in, check-out

Your Security Officers will need two tables either side of the detection frame to use for all of the registration administration. You can use normal tables and cover them in foil for that space look.

Main Spaceship

Walls

The darker the walls of your venue the better, because then you can cover them in silver/gold/glitter/stars/planets/glow-in-the-dark shapes. You may want to cover the walls in black material.

Portholes x 5

If you cut long strips of 127 mm-(5 inch)-wide card, and then cut some curved corner sections, you will be ready to assemble your portholes on the walls. If you have time you can either cover them in trusty silver foil or spray-paint them silver. They will easily stick to the wall with sticky tack. Make sure they're all basically the same size but you can experiment with different shapes.

Stage area

If you don't have an actual stage then getting hold of some stage blocks would be a good idea. If it's not practical or you feel it's unnecessary because of the size of your club, then mark out the 'stage' using masking tape or – even better – silver gaffer tape! This will clearly show the kids where their boundaries are. The equipment also needs to be kept away from little hands and needs to be topple-over safe! The overhead projector (OHP) screen should be placed at the back in the middle of the stage. You need to create a Spaceship Control Room on the stage – specifically for Captain Smirk and Lieutenant Savoy. Here are some suggestions: old TV screens placed in a row on a table covered in black material; painted cardboard boxes with brightly coloured buttons, a brightly coloured swivel chair for the captain and a stool for the lieutenant.

Beam spot

If you want something simple and quick, just mark the middle of the room with a cross of gaffer tape (preferably silver!). If you want something slightly more complicated, cover a small stool, or an upside-down crate, in silver foil.

Engine Rooms 1 and 2

You will need clear signs for the doors, showing which room is for which group. Other than that you don't need to do much in regards to decoration unless you feel inspired.

Promote It!

So you've decided you're going to run *Mission: Miracle Maker*, you've got a team of people ready to help; all you need now is some children to come! There are two main ways you can advertise your holiday club.

Local churches. It might be an idea to ask to visit all your local churches and do a five-minute presentation about the holiday club. If you're also in need of extra helpers you could use this opportunity to ask. Be creative with the presentation. For example, if you've got people who are good at drama they could maybe go as Captain Smirk and Lieutenant Savoy and do a short sketch, inviting the children to come.

Local primary schools. Obviously if you have children in your church then some of them will go to some of the schools you want to visit, so you could maybe ask the parents to approach the school on your behalf. Hopefully you'll find that the headteacher will let you have a short slot in an assembly and then the children could have a letter that's put in all the registers. Again, be creative if you can – you want something that will whet their appetite!

Promotion Material

There is a range of promotional publicity material available to purchase from CPO, including banners, posters and invitations (see back of book for details). If you are running a very small event, and will only need a very limited supply of promotional material, there are logos, sample posters and invitations included on the CD for you to use (full details on the CD itself). Make sure that on your publicity it's totally clear who is running the club, parents will want to know that it is a legitimate event. If you don't want to have your home phone number as the contact number then why not have your church number and make sure that whoever works in the office knows all about the club and is happy to take enquiries on your behalf.

Legal Stuff

Child Protection Policy!

Do you really need one?

YES!

If you don't have one, your insurance may be invalid. By law anyone employed to look after children under 18 has to make a signed declaration of any criminal record. It is recommended that your volunteers do this as well, because if any child came to harm (this includes ill treatments of any kind – including sexual abuse, or impairment of physical or mental health or development) due to any of your leaders, this could lead to a claim of negligence.

Does your church/organisation have a CPP?

Yes = Then it's wise for your leaders to follow the established process.

No = Why not?! This is a good reason to set one up, then. If you need any help, contact the Churches Child Protection Advisory Service on 01322 667207 or 01322 660011.

So what next?

Well, get your leader to sign a declaration like the one on page 7.

What about police checks?

It costs £10 for the police to do a check on a person to see if they have a criminal record. Although it is not a legal requirement, we would recommend you ask your leaders to organise this themselves. This would mean they could use them for any children's/youth work in the future. A person just needs to go into their local police station and ask for the form, allowing a few weeks for police checks to be processed.

What about social services?

You may need to register with the local social services. Phone them up and speak to the local daycare advisor.

Some things to consider ...

Be aware that checking is quite a sensitive issue. Make sure your leaders know that you aren't accusing them of anything – it is a positive procedure.

Be careful with any information that your leaders give you. If you are in any doubt about a particular person, discuss it with a respected Christian leader.

It might be a good idea to ask your leader for a referee or two. Here are some questions you could ask if you do:

How long have you known .... ?

How do you know .... ?

How willing is .... to work in a team?

What are ....'s best personality traits?

Would you consider .... suitable to work with children and young people?

Are there any relevant details about .... that may cause concern?

CONFIDENTIAL DECLARATION

Guidelines from the Home Office following the Children's Act 1989 advise that all voluntary organisations, including churches, take steps to safeguard the children who are in their care. You are therefore asked to make the following declarations:

Do you have any current or spent criminal convictions, cautions, bindovers or cases pending?

Yes ☐ No ☐

Have you ever been held liable by a court under the Rehabilitation of Offenders Act 1974 for a civil wrong, or had an order made against you by a matrimonial or a family court?

Yes ☐ No ☐

Has your conduct ever caused, or been likely to cause harm to a child or put a child at risk, or, to your knowledge, has it ever been alleged that your conduct has resulted in any of these things?

Yes ☐ No ☐

Signed____Date______________

Because of the nature of the work for which you are applying, this post is exempt from the provision of section 4(ii) of the Rehabilitation of Offenders Act 1974, by virtue of the Rehabilitation of Offenders Act 1974 (Exemptions) Order 1975, and you are therefore not entitled to withhold information about convictions which, for other purposes are 'spent' under the provisions of the Act. In the event of an appointment, any failure to disclose such convictions could result in the withdrawal of approval to work with children in the church.

Video Licence

If you plan to show the full-length clips of the video as suggested in the day's introduction you will be showing the whole film over the course of the week and will therefore need to obtain a licence from the Bible Society.

If however you choose to shorten the length of the section of film shown each day, and the total amount of clips do not exceed 15 minutes during the week, then you do not need to obtain a licence.

How do I obtain a licence?

Write to: Kathryn Ruddle, Rights Administrator, Bible Society, Stonehill Green, Westlea, Swindon, SN5 7DE.

Include your name, address and church details, date and venue of showing, and state it is for the Topz Holiday Club.

The charge for the licence will be £30, payable after the event.

Order, Order!

Anyone who has ever worked with children will know that they need some boundaries to their behaviour! It's important that you have some sort of basic rules for your club, and there are some suggested rules below. You will need to make sure that everyone who is helping to run the club is aware of these rules. Inevitably with rules in place there will be some who end up breaking them, so you'll also need to have some sort of discipline procedure in place. Again you will need to make sure all the leaders are aware of this. In our experience it's probably best to have one or two people who are ultimately in charge of enforcing discipline. This takes the responsibility away from leaders who may be less experienced at working with children.

An easy system for discipline that we've found works quite well with this age group is a red and yellow card system. As in the game of football, if a child breaks one of the rules they then receive a first warning; if a further rule is broken they receive a yellow card; and then, if they still can't behave and break the rules again, they receive a red card. It's up to you to decide what a red card means; it could mean anything from they're not allowed to join in the next game or activity and have to sit with a leader to they're not allowed back the next day.

All this can seem quite negative so you could also have a reward scheme where throughout the morning you give out 'Snonge Tokens', which can then be traded at the end of the session for sweets. You could award these tokens for anything you want, e.g. if someone helps you, if someone smiles a lot or wins a game. All they need to be is either circular card or a different colour (i.e. not yellow or red) square card. You could put the *Millennium Parrot* logo on if you wanted and laminate them if you're really keen!

So here are some suggested *Mission: Miracle Maker* rules:

Listen carefully. Whenever a member of the *Millennium Parrot* crew is talking to you, either on your own or in the big group, you should stop talking, and listen to them.

Show respect. Treat everyone on board the ship well. No name-calling, fighting or damaging other people's property.

Have fun! Be ready to join in with all the games and activities without complaining. This will also help others to have fun.

Emergency Smergency!

This is designed to be a bit of fun and the idea is that the children never know when it might happen. It can also be used if there is an actual emergency, but hopefully that won't happen. On the CD enclosed is the sound of a siren. Basically at any time each morning this siren can be sounded and then everyone has to drop everything and gather at the allocated point (this can be decided by you). They will then receive a series of commands, all at random, at which they have to do the relevant actions.

Here are the commands:

Port	All move to the left of the hall
Starboard	All move to the right of the hall
Meteor	Everyone gets into a tight ball
Captain on Board	Do Snonge salute, which is where you put your hands on your ears and waggle the fingers
Warp Speed	Everyone has to link arms
Low Oxygen	Put your hands over your mouth like a mask and move very slowly
Yellow Alert	Everyone cries out, 'Oh no!'
Red Alert	Everyone cries out, 'Oh no, I'm scared!'
Laser Beam	Everyone sits around the beam spot, facing inwards
Heat Overload	Everyone goes outside quietly (to a specified area) and lines up in their two groups, where the crew do a head count to make sure everyone is there. The Security Officers should have a list of who is there each day. Make sure you do this one on the first day.
Satellite	Everyone sits facing the stage with their arms outstretched. You can use this each time you want the children to be ready to watch a sketch.

To help the children remember which is which, you could have lists of the commands at various places around the spaceship. Or you could practise some commands at an appropriate time each morning.

Equipment Needed

Mission: Miracle Maker has been written so you could run it with very little equipment. However, if you can get your hands on some slightly more flashy equipment it would be good. So below are our suggestions for equipment you could use.

Visual

Overhead projector and screen (or wall to project on) – Obviously you'll need to make sure that the lighting in the venue will allow you to see what is being projected.
Video – To create more of a cinema effect, a video projector would be the ideal way to show the daily video clips. However, these really need to go through some sort of public address (PA) system, which not everyone will have. So if you can't do that then you can use a good old TV and video player.

Audio

PA – To a certain extent it depends on the size of the group as to whether you need to use a PA or not. If you have more than ten children we do recommend that you have some sort of PA. If you have musicians who are going to play for the *Mission: Miracle Maker* song you will need to make sure the PA is capable of taking that many inputs. Having a PA also means that you will need someone who knows how to set it up and operate it!
CD player – If you're going to use the CD enclosed with this book you will obviously need a CD player. If you're using a PA then you will need to check that the CD player has the right outputs so it can be put through the PA. You will also need a way of playing music for some of the games.

Lighting

Spotlight – This is entirely optional but it would look quite good if you had a spotlight for the 'Beam me up, Swotty' section.
House lights – If you're using videos and an OHP then you do need to make sure that the main lighting in the room won't intrude too much. You may need to ask someone to dim down the lights when needed.

Checklist for Each Day – Have you got all you need?

- Snonge Space Passport for each child *(sample on page 14)*
- Passport stamp for Check-in
- *Mission: Miracle Maker* CD for King Snorg's transmission, Emergency Smergency siren, *Mission: Miracle Maker* Song and Swotty's jingle
- Spare music CDs – Space themed/children's songs/popular music
- Acetate of King Snorg
- Acetate of the words of the *Mission: Miracle Maker* song
- *The Miracle Maker* video
- Props box: logbook, packed lunch (sandwiches, comet cola [also for Swotty to use], Mars bar), box of tissues, matchbox, empty glass bottle with tomato ketchup label, hand-held microphone for Swotty
- Costumes for actors
- Refreshments – we recommend you keep this simple (e.g. squash and biscuits)
- Tuck shop (if you're having one)
- Snonge Tokens for rewards (if you're using them)
- Yellow and red cards for discipline (if you're using them)
- Craft materials – glue, sellotape, scissors, pens, pencils, crayons, paint, brushes, etc.
- Activity worksheets for each child (if needed)
- Homequest for each child
- First-aid kit
- Accident/incident book
- Costumes/uniforms for all the crew
- Activity materials – these are listed with each activity.

Letter to Parent/Guardian

Church/Christian Organisation
Address
Telephone
E-mail

Date

Dear parents/guardian

We are running a holiday club/activity week/weekly club for 5- to 11-year-olds called *Mission: Miracle Maker.*
Here are the details:

Date:
Time:
Venue:

Refreshments will be provided but your child may want to bring some money for the tuck shop.

Your child has expressed an interest. If you are happy for your child to take part, please fill in the enclosed Permission Form and send it back to us.

We will then contact you to confirm that your child has a place. If you have any queries please do contact us.

We look forward to seeing your child at *Mission: Miracle Maker.*

Your Name:
Mission: Miracle Maker team leader

Mission: Miracle Maker

PERMISSION FORM

Full name of child ______________________________

Male/female ______________________________

Date of birth ______________________________

Address ______________________________

______________________________ Postcode ______________

Telephone number ______________________________

Emergency or Parent/Guardian mobile telephone number ______________

Other important information about child? ______________________________

____

____

Date ______________________________

School and class ______________________________

______________________________ Age ______________

GP's name and telephone number ______________________________

____

Known allergies/conditions ______________________________

____

I authorise only ______________________________ to collect my child
(We will need any notification of change to this to be in writing.)

Signature of parent/guardian ______________________________

Adult's name printed ______________________________

In the unlikely event of illness or accident I give permission for any necessary medical treatment to be given by the nominated first aider. In an emergency and if I am not contactable I am willing for my son/daughter to receive hospital treatment, including anaesthetic.

The Crew

Have You Got Enough Help?!

For children aged three to eight years, you will need one leader to eight children; and for children aged over eight years, you will need one leader to twelve children – this is a legal requirement. We suggest you have a simple costume/uniform for the crew to identify themselves to the kids and their parents/guardians. This can be very easily done, with just plain dark trousers or jeans and matching T-shirts. Have a look at the CPO printed T-shirts at the back of this book. We also recommend that all the crew gather together at the beginning and end of the morning for a briefing and prayer time.

Here is a list of roles you, as the coordinator, will need to delegate.

Security Officers (two at least needed)

These will be in charge of registration, ensuring that each child has a signed permission form, passing on any medication (for which permission has been given by the parent/guardian), handing out the Snonge Space Passports and stamping them each day the child comes to the club. They need to keep a list of all the kids at the club each day. You will also need to work out a suitable system for safe 'check-out' and collection of children at the end of the day. If practical it may be a good idea for the SOs to stay at their desks throughout the session – in case there are latecomers or unnamed visitors, and also to chat with and get to know the parents/guardians. Suggested costume: security-style hats, crew T-shirt, and name badge.

Stitch

This person is the allocated first-aider (in charge of the first-aid kit). We recommend that they also be in charge of the accident/incident book. Should a child be injured, Stitch should record the date, time, how it happened, who was involved, and what action was taken, together with a counter-signature. Stitch needs to be easily identifiable; you could possibly put this person in a crew T-shirt with a red cross on it, plus a hat, also with a red cross on it.

Musicians

You may want a small band to play the song and teach it. Otherwise you will need a couple of people who are confident at singing to teach the song to the children, using the CD.

Super Rocket Actors

There are a variety of sketches each day. The roles are as follows:

King Snorg

Sends the children on the mission. You can either use the CD provided, or read the script out while the King Snorg picture goes on the OHP. No costume needed.

Captain Smirk and Lieutenant Savoy

Each day they lead the session through, ensuring that the timings for the activities are kept, teaching the song and so on. They also perform a sketch that vaguely introduces the theme for the session, and lead the Emergency Smergencies. Suggested costume: *Thunderbirds*-style jacket, over a crew T-shirt, and a *Thunderbirds*-style hat.

Swotty

A game-show-host-style interviewer – in a sketch each session. Suggested costume: Sparkly jacket, over a crew T-shirt, hand-held microphone, comet cola bottle (which should look something like a cola bottle) and possibly sunglasses. Can be either male or female.

Biblical Characters (five needed)

Each day Swotty interviews a biblical character about their experience of Jesus' miraculous powers.

Day 1 – Mary (mother of Jesus); suggested costume: white dress with red cloth over shoulders
Day 2 – Simon Peter; suggested costume: beard (painted on?), grey tunic with blue cloth around waist.

Day 3 – Tabitha (lady healed of internal bleeding); suggested costume: white tunic dress with thin blue stripes
Day 4 – Lazarus; suggested costume: beige tunic, bandages, beard, long brown waistcoat, white Jewish skullcap
Day 5 – Mary Magdalene, suggested costume: turquoise tunic dress, red cloak and white cloth around waist.

(If necessary two characters can be played by the same person.) Don't worry about actors looking exactly like the characters in the video!

Satellite Prayer Team

They will meet together to pray for the club while it is happening. You could have core members; then others can join them for a shorter length of time. You will need to pass on prayer requests, maybe write down the children's names. Set up the prayer room as creatively as you want – with paper, pens, CD player and worship CDs. It would be a good idea to ask them to arrive 30 minutes early to pray with and for the crew.

Training Sessions

It's really important to meet with your crew a few weeks before (whenever is most practical). You may need to have two shorter sessions to fit it all in, or one longer session – perhaps a day at the weekend.

Icebreaker – Have a bit of fun by playing a game and learning the song!
Pray, and get a mission statement – Why are you doing it? What are your hopes and expectations?
Legal stuff – Explain about Child Protection guidelines.
Session timings – There is a lot in every session so your crew will have to be on the ball, ready to move to the next part at the right time!
Who's who? – Explain the different roles and decide who's taking them. Make sure they are clear who they are responsible to and that they know that they are not alone.
First aid – Introduce the first-aider, who will then need to explain the procedure for accidents.
Emergency procedures – Explain about Emergency Smergency, particularly the fire exit procedure.
How to lead children – Give the crew an idea of the kind of things to expect – perhaps you could do some role plays. It's likely that for some this will be the first time they've worked with children. Here are some of the things we suggest you cover:

- Avoid using Christian jargon that unchurched kids won't understand
- Build good relationships with the kids
- Be as positive as possible
- Avoid being tactile, and always pray/talk to a child in an area where others are present and you can be clearly seen
- Explain the procedure to use if a child discloses some information
- Look out for the loners and shy ones but also make sure you give time to the slightly more 'troublesome' ones
- Try not to label them
- Give them a chance to prove themselves
- Get the best out of them
- Try to learn their names – it can mean a lot to them
- Remember your focus is the kids – don't stand around chatting to your mates and, most importantly
- LOVE the kids!

Thespians are us! – Give out scripts and if you've got time, split up into groups to rehearse and decide on costumes. Those not involved can watch and give helpful advice!
Follow-up work – Are you having any? Do crew members want to be involved?
Pray again – What are people's worries? Pray for individuals and for the children coming to the club.

Mission:
Miracle Maker

Snonge
Space Passport

Name:

___

Age:

___

Favourite food:

___

Favourite colour:

___

Spaceship travelling on:

Galaxy Chicken/Millennium Parrot/
Nebuli Sparrow III

(delete as appropriate)

Starbuster ☐

Moonraker ☐

(Tick which one)

Signature

___

Mission: Miracle Maker Song Words

Chorus

We're on a mission mission mission mission mission *(Count on fingers and thumbs)*
To find the miracle miracle miracle miracle maker *(Count on fingers and thumbs)*
We're on a mission mission mission mission mission *(Count on fingers and thumbs)*
To find the Miracle Man. *(Windmill arms)*

Verse 1

We've been searching the stars, 'Whoosh!' *(Right-hand rocket)*
Passing Venus and Mars, 'Peee-ow!' *(Left-hand rocket)*
On board *(Clap hands x 2)*
The *Millennium (Clap hands x 2)*
Parrot, 'Pieces of Eight'. *(Parrot hand)*

We're gonna learn all we can, 'Oh, yeah!' *(Scribble hand)*
About the Miracle Man, 'He's amazing!' *(Windmill arms)*
On board *(Clap hands x 2)*
The *Millennium (Clap hands x 2)*
Parrot, 'Pieces of Eight'. *(Parrot hand)*

Chorus

Verse 2

Planet Earth is in sight, 'Where?' *(Binocular hands)*
We need to find out what's right, 'That's right!' *(Thumbs up)*
It's us *(Stamp feet x 2)*
And all *(Stamp feet x 2)*
The crew, 'High Five'. *(High five)*

And when our mission is done, 'Ping' *(Turn around on spot)*
We'll have had lots of fun, 'Spacetastic!' *(Snonge Salute)*
With us *(Stamp feet x 2)*
And all *(Stamp feet x 2)*
The crew, 'High Five'. *(High five)*

Chorus

Refrain

His name is Jesus
And He cares for you
He changes lives
If you want Him to.

Chorus

Mission: Miracle Maker Song Music

Emma Smallwood & Jeni Wilson

G A D
on board the Mill - e - ni - um Par - rot.
on board the Mill - e - ni - um Par - rot.
1.
2.
D.C.
G D7
We're gon - na
ch: We're on a
His name is Je - sus,
G A D G D7
and He cares for you.
He chang - es li - ves
E7 A
D.C.
G A
if you want Him to!
ch: We're on a
to find the Mir a - cle Man.
D G A D
to find the Mir a - cle Man.

You can photocopy King Snorg onto an OHP from this page to show during his transmission (colour and black and white versions available on the CD).

God becomes human!

DAY 1

Aim of Today's Session
(Matthew 1:18 – 2:11)

Today we will be looking at the miracle of God becoming human. Several characters are introduced in the video but we want to focus on Jesus' birth. It's quite a difficult concept to understand, even when you're old and wrinkly, so when we talk to younger children we need to be as clear and simple as possible.

Avoid talking about the 'Immaculate Conception' and other complicated issues. By the end of today, the children should be able to understand that Jesus had a human mother and a heavenly Father and He was so important that we still celebrate His birth at Christmas time.

Approximate Timings

9.15	Crew Countdown – Crew and Satellite Prayer Team meet together. Brief them and pray
9.45	Check-in – Security Officers give out Snonge Passports to kids and stamp the first day. Play music as they arrive. Crew should mingle with the children and chat to them
10.00	King Snorg's Transmission. He sends the kids on a mission
10.05	Crew sketch – includes rules, emergency smergency, introduction to the crew and *Mission: Miracle Maker* song
10.25	Game – Pass the Meteor
10.40	*The Miracle Maker* video clip
11.00	Activity 1 – Making Alien Masks
11.20	Refreshment break
11.30	'Beam Me Up, Swotty' – Guest star: Mary, mother of Jesus
11.35	Activity 2 – Split into Moonrakers and Starbusters
11.55	Round up the day, explain Check-out procedure. Each child has to give their passport to the Security Officers. They cannot go until they are told to go, one person at a time. Distribute Homequest sheets
12.00	End of session. Crew debrief and prayer

The Miracle Maker Video Clip
Synopsis (0 hr 0 mins – 0 hr 15 mins)

We are introduced to the character of Tamar (Jairus' daughter), who watches the busy scene in Galilee. She sees Jesus working as a carpenter. We also meet Mary Magdalene as she wanders through the streets talking to herself. Tamar is told to come away by her father, who is worried about her health. Jesus goes home to His mother Mary; they talk about when He was a boy. Jesus tells her that He is leaving in the morning. As Mary sleeps she remembers when He was born. Jesus then goes to the River Jordan where He is baptised by His cousin John, after which He is tempted by the devil in the desert. Jesus goes to visit His friend Lazarus and Lazarus' two sisters Mary and Martha. He explains that He is no longer building doors but He is building the kingdom of God.

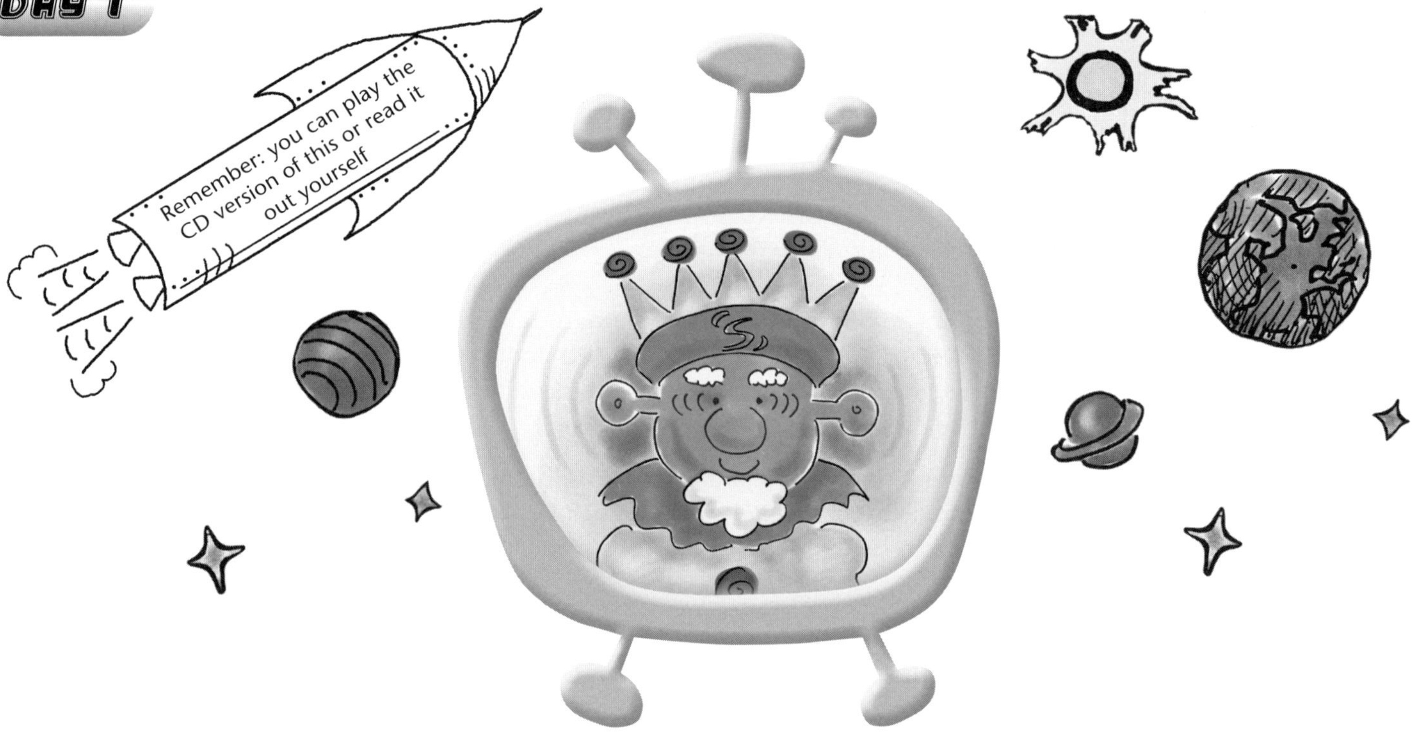

King Snorg's Transmission

Greetings, intrepid space explorers! My name is King Snorg of Snonge and I would like to thank you all, on behalf of everyone on the planet Snonge, for agreeing to take part in this mission, codenamed Miracle Maker. For many light years now we have been fascinated with life on the planet you call Earth but it was only recently that we heard about some strange goings-on in a little-known part of that planet, called Galilee in the country of Israel.

One of our new recruits, Private SnugglePuss the Third, was returning to Snonge following a successful mission to collect cheese from the moon when he got lost and ended up on the planet Earth. Through some strange space twist he'd also gone back in time 2,000 years to AD 30. The part of the Earth he landed on was called Israel.

Now poor SnugglePuss was very bedraggled having crashed his ship, but he was a professional and he knew the first thing he had to do was refuel his ship, but this was difficult to start with. The locals had never heard of petrol, let alone hyperlite fuel, the advanced fuel we use on Snonge. SnugglePuss went to see a local chariot manufacturer, called Ofire. After a few days of experimenting with possible alternative fuel sources they discovered that donkey manure might just work. However, it was rather a long shot. They needed a bit of help from someone who knew more about this kind of thing. Ofire told SnugglePuss that there was a man who lived in that area who could apparently do amazing miracles – rumour had it that He could turn water into wine! They decided that they would find this 'Miracle Maker' and ask for His help.

But on the day before they were due to set off to find the 'Miracle Maker', Ofire the chariot maker was messing around in the workshop when he discovered that, if you mixed donkey manure and sand together and then heated it up, it gave off a gas similar to the gas of hyperlite fuel. Eager to get back to his home, Snonge, Private SnugglePuss quickly prepared the ship for take-off while Ofire loaded the fuel on board. They said their goodbyes and SnugglePuss disappeared into outer space once more. He eventually found his way back to Snonge where everybody was keen to hear all about his exploits and, of course, taste the lovely cheese he got from the moon! The main thing we were curious about, though, was this 'Miracle Maker' and we decided that we needed to go back and gather as much information as we could about Him.

This is where you all come in. We want you to spend the next five days in the Earth's orbit where you will all have a chance to spend time looking at evidence gathered by the crew members. You are to find out as much as you can about this 'Miracle Maker' and report back to the crew as soon as you find anything.

Thank you all once again. Good luck! I look forward to hearing all about it.

Goodbye!

Crew Sketch

Characters: ***Captain Smirk, Lieutenant Savoy***

Props: ***Logbook***

Captain: Welcome on board the *Millennium Parrot*. I am Captain Smirk and I am your … Captain *(realises it's obvious)*. This is Lieutenant Savoy.

Lieutenant: Hello.

Captain: It's our job to guide you on this very important mission. The *Millennium Parrot* is the largest vessel of the Snonge Star Fleet and we look forward to travelling with you all. Before we get our mission under way we need to teach you the Emergency Smergency procedure. When you hear this noise *(play Siren noise)* you all need to quickly and quietly come and gather here *(show them where you want them to go)*. Then when we say certain words you have to do certain things! For example, when I say, 'Port', you all move to this side of the room *(point them to the left of the room)*. Let's do that now. Port! *(all move to left of room)*. Then if I say, 'Starboard', you all move to this side of the room *(point them to the right of the room)*. Let's do that now. Starboard! *(all move to the right of room)*. (*You then need to do the same for all the other Emergency Smergency commands, especially the 'Heat Overload' command, which is in effect your fire drill.*)
OK! We're getting the hang of Emergency Smergency now, good. Now I know we're going to have lots of fun on our mission but we need simple rules to help us have the maximum amount of fun. (*You will then need to explain your* ***Mission: Miracle Maker*** *rules and also your reward system if you have one.*)
Right, we've got all that out of the way. Now we're at the start of our mission, codename 'Miracle', so we'd like to sing our little song. Join in when you can, it's very easy. *(Teach song.)*
Well done, everyone. By the end of the week we should all know it off by heart.

Lieutenant: Erm, Captain …

Captain: Hang on a second, Lieutenant. I've nearly finished.

Lieutenant: But, Captain, I've just noticed something.

Captain: Well, it'd better be good, Lieutenant. I'm supposed to start off this voyage by giving a full briefing.

Lieutenant: Well, I've just been looking through the ship's log and it appears today is a very special day.

Captain: It is? Oh, my goodness, it's not my mum's birthday, is it? I forgot it last year! Oh, please tell me …

Lieutenant: No, no, no, Captain, it's not your mother's birthday.

Captain: Phew!

Lieutenant: But you're close.

Captain: Oh, well, um … it's not … your birthday?

Lieutenant: No, Captain, it's not. Do you really think I'd forget my own birthday? And I certainly wouldn't let you forget it was mine!

Captain: No, that's true! So what day is it? C'mon, you've got me worried now.

Lieutenant: It's St Snonge Day!

Captain: What! Today?

Lieutenant: Yes!

Captain: I can't believe we forgot St Snonge Day. Why didn't anyone remind me?

Lieutenant: Well, the intergalactic communication systems have had a bit of a virus.

Captain: Well, there has been a nasty flu bug going round …

Lieutenant: No, not that kind of virus. A computer virus, which has meant our communication with Snonge has been limited.

Captain: Oh, well, what do you suggest we do? We don't want all these wonderful people to miss putting on the celebrations. After all, it is the day we remember when Samuel Snonge first discovered our planet …

Lieutenant: I know, I know. Let me think …

Captain: Could you maybe think a little faster …

Lieutenant: I've got it! You know how on Snonge we all wear masks and play Pass the Meteor? Well, we could get them all to do that!

Captain: What a splendid idea! Let's do it!

Lieutenant: Why don't we play Pass the Meteor first, then do the masks later?

Captain: OK. Let's get on with it!

Game

Pass the Meteor

For each meteor you will need: a prize, layers of paper, sweets, forfeits and music

As the name suggests, this game is a very simple variation on the popular party game, Pass the Parcel. You will need to prepare at least one meteor; a second or third if you have a large number of children in the club. The meteor needs to have a prize (ideally space-related), which is wrapped up in lots of different layers of paper. In between the different layers you could include extra small prizes, e.g. sweets, and/or for a little more entertainment value you could write some forfeits (you might need to have two different forfeits – one for the Starbusters and one for the Moonrakers). The outside layer of the meteor should be covered either in grey paper or in white paper painted grey. The children sit round in a circle. Music is then played and the children pass the meteor around the circle. When the music stops the person holding the meteor gets to remove a layer of paper. They then either win the prize or have to do the forfeit.

Activity 1

Alien Masks

You will need: paper plates – one for each person, scissors, string or elastic, felt-tip pens, glitter, fabric, wool, paints, pipe cleaners, milk bottle tops, etc. to decorate mask, glue

Give each child a paper plate. The leaders will then need to help the children mark on their paper plates where their eyes would go and cut them out. Then the children design and decorate their own Alien Mask. You will need to provide them with materials to do this. Once the masks are dry you can attach string or elastic to them so they can wear them. Don't give the masks to them today, though, as it looks really good if you make a display of them in Porthole 1 of the Spaceship. If they put their names on them, they can take them home at the end of the week.

Activity 2

At this point in the morning, ideally you want to split your group into two groups, 5- to 7-year-olds and 8- to 11-year-olds. This means you will need leaders to go with each.

Starbusters

You will need: paper, pencils, pens

Tell them a story about Bernard, the little boy who, one day while watching some ants crawling around, began to wonder what it would be like to be an ant. He tried to make himself as small as an ant, and found out what ants eat but still didn't know. He asked his mum and dad and they didn't know either. So Bernard decided that at school on Monday he would ask his teacher, Mrs Golding. She always knew things. So just as everyone was going to lunch Bernard went over to Mrs Golding and asked. She had a long hard think and then finally told him that really the only way Bernard could know what it was like to be an ant was to actually become one. Bernard was a bit disappointed but deep down quite relieved because he was quite happy being a little boy!

Use this story to explain that one of the reasons God became a little baby and then grew up to be a man was so that He would know what it was like to be human. Recap on the part of the story of Jesus' birth where the wise men gave Jesus gifts. Get them to think: if Jesus was born today, what gift would they give Him. Then get them to draw a picture of it. You'll then put all their pictures on the wall.

Moonrakers

You will need: a Maze Puzzle for each child **(master on p.23 or as pdf on CD)**

Ask them to think about ants. Ask the question, 'If you wanted to know what it was like to be an ant, what could you do to find out?' Discuss their answers. If they haven't already said, explain that the best way to know what it's like is to actually become an ant. Then ask the questions, 'Would anyone like to be an ant for a day?' and 'Would anyone like to become an ant forever?' Discuss their answers. Explain that one of the reasons God came to live on earth as a human being was so He would know what it's like for us. Recap on the bit in the video where Jesus got left behind by Mary and Joseph. Then get them to help Jesus find His way through the maze to find Joseph and Mary.

Spend a couple of minutes praying with them, thanking God for sending Jesus to live on earth.

Activity 2 – Moonrakers

OK, Moonrakers, we need your help. Jesus has been separated from Mary & Joseph. Can you find your way through the maze and help them get back together again? Have a go now!

Beam Me Up, Swotty

While the children are having their refreshments, Mary positions herself on the beam spot. The Siren goes off and the Captain and Lieutenant shout, 'Laser Beam!' so that the children sit around the beam spot. As the jingle plays, Swotty appears.

Swotty: Hello and welcome to 'Beam Me Up, Swotty' – sponsored by Comet Cola – the drink that makes you go 'PING' *(holds up a can)*. The show where we beam up special people from other planets. This week we are going to the planet Earth at a very amazing time in the planet's history – a time that the humans call 'around AD 30' and to a place they call 'Israel'. Now each time we do this I have absolutely no idea who will be arriving – which makes it all the more exciting. This week our 'Beamed People' have been chosen by Private SnugglePuss the Third himself, who has been visiting the planet recently. He keeps going back actually ... I've heard he's been thinking of getting a holiday home there. Anyway let's not waste any more time and get on with meeting our first Beamer of the Week. In case you haven't seen the show before, at this point I need some help from you. Yes, you, and you *(he points at a few children)* in fact all of you. Now when I say 'Starbusters, Moonrakers, what are we waiting for?', I want you to say, 'Swotty, we're ready, who are we waiting for?' OK, has everyone got that? Let's practise. Starbusters, Moonrakers, what are we waiting for? *(kids reply)*. OK. Let's go for the real thing now, and by the time we've finished saying it our Beamer should have fully arrived! Ready? OK. Starbusters, Moonrakers what are we waiting for? *(Kids reply. Mary begins to move slowly. She is a little confused as to where she is. Speaking to Mary)* Hello, welcome to my show, 'Beam Me Up, Swotty' – sponsored by Comet Cola, the drink that makes you go 'PING'! How are you feeling? I know that beaming can be quite tiring – I always get a headache.

Mary: I'm fine, thank you.

Swotty: So what's your name and where d'you come from?

Mary: Erm ... my name's Mary and I'm from Israel.

Swotty: Well, Mary, can you tell us a little about yourself?

Mary: What would you like to know?

Swotty: Let me see, do you have a job?

Mary: No, well, I've got a husband and a family to look after.

Swotty: Ah, a husband! What's his name then? Tell us a bit about him.

Mary: His name is Joseph. He's a hard-working, honest, lovely man. He's a carpenter, you know. He makes things out of wood, like chairs and tables. We've been happily married for many, many years now.

Swotty: *(puts his finger in his ear as if he's got an earpiece)* Now, I'm being told by my director, who obviously knows a bit more about you than I do, that it wasn't a very happy start to your marriage. He says it was very unusual. Can you tell us about that, Mary?

Mary: Well it wasn't unhappy but it was a little unusual, I suppose. You see, I'd known Joe ever since I was young and we got to know each other after my father asked him to make a chest of drawers for my cousin's wedding present. He was around our house quite a bit – my parents liked him. So anyway we got engaged and soon after I had a visit from an angel. He told me I was going to have a son but that it wouldn't be Joe's!

Swotty: *(cough)* Had you been seeing someone else then?

Mary: No. Not at all! I was very much in love with Joe. We brought Him up together but His actual Father was God.

Swotty: Hang on a satellite-second! You were engaged and then an angel said you were going to have God's Son? And then you did?

Mary: Yes.

Swotty: How did Joseph feel about this?

Mary: I think he was a little confused at first, but he accepted it. An angel spoke to him in a dream and told him not to worry, to carry on and marry me, and to call the child Jesus.

Swotty: Wow! Another angel!

Mary: Actually there were more when the baby was born.

Swotty: What did the angels tell you this time?

Mary: They didn't come to see me and Joe – they spoke to some people out in fields near where we were. They told them that the baby who had been born was a king and to go and visit him.

Swotty: Oh, so you're royalty. *(He begins to bow)* I've always wanted to meet royalty.

Mary: No, no, not me – just Jesus.

Swotty: So King Jesus made sure you and Joe were all right for money and stuff, did He?

Mary: He's not that sort of a king! When He was born we had to stay in an animal shed, out the back of a house because we had nowhere else to go.

Swotty: An animal shed! He really is a different kind of king, isn't He, your son Jesus? Well, I'd love to talk to you for hours, Mary, but our time has run out, unfortunately. Thank you so much for being on the show. Just to sum up – our Beamer of the Day was Mary from Israel at the time of 'around AD 30'. She had a son called Jesus, who was also the Son of God. It truly is a miracle! Thank you for being a wonderful audience – see you again tomorrow. Let's give Mary a big round of applause and beam her back to earth.

(As the audience claps, Mary waves on the spot but slowly begins to freeze. The jingle plays and Swotty waves goodbye to the audience and goes off. Do a couple of Emergency Smergencies before moving into Activity 2, during which Mary disappears.)

DAY 1

M:MM Homequest

After all the excitement of today it's time to go home … sad but true. But you can still do some investigation about the Miracle Maker on your own at home … Yippee! Every day you can take home a 'Homequest' and the Topz Gang will be helping you along the way! Today Dave is going to tell us what we've got to do. So take it away, Dave!

Hi everyone, I'm Dave Howell and I'm part of the Topz Gang. There are seven of us and we're all really good friends. We're all Christians too so we think following Jesus is just 'Topz'!!! I live with my mum and dad and when I'm not at school I love to go out on my bike. I bet some of you like cycling too! Can any of you remember what today's miracle was? In case you've forgotten, here's the answer, only it's written backwards so you might need a mirror!

God became a human being called Jesus

Did you get that? Now, how good are you at remembering things? The story about Jesus we looked at today is written in the Bible in a book called Matthew. There's a short sentence that helps us to remember how amazing it is that God became a human. Why don't you see if you can learn it before the next ***Mission: Miracle Maker*** *session? Here it is …*

'They will call him Immanuel – which means, God with us.'

Now, just for a bit of fun, here's a wordsearch all about Jesus' birth for you to do. See if you can find all the words … have fun!

BABY	*GIFT*
MARY	*SHEPHERDS*
ANGELS	*GOD*
JOSEPH	*STAR*
MIRACLE	*BETHLEHEM*
WISE MEN	

D	E	L	C	A	R	I	M	M
B	A	B	Y	P	M	R	B	S
G	E	O	D	X	S	A	R	H
O	I	T	N	W	Y	T	B	B
G	I	F	H	P	E	S	O	J
D	A	T	S	L	O	R	Y	L
S	H	E	P	H	E	R	D	S
E	F	D	W	T	A	H	P	D
J	O	S	H	M	F	D	E	Y
G	N	E	M	E	S	I	W	M
A	A	N	G	E	L	S	G	D

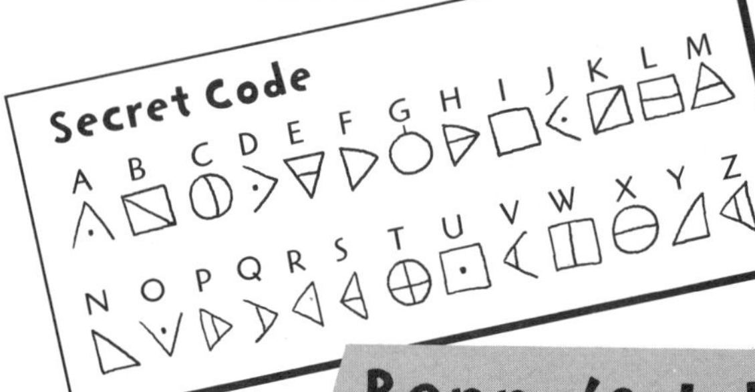

Benny's Joke

Hi there! I'm Benny – and I'm the joker of the Gang. I'll be telling you a joke every day – but you'll have to work out the answer using the special Topz code. Have fun – and we'll see you tomorrow.

How do you get a baby astronaut to sleep?

Jesus can even control the fish!

Aim of Today's Session
(Luke 5:1 - 11)

Today we will be looking at the story of the miraculous catch of fish. The key point of this miracle is that people never tried to catch fish in the middle of the day because the fish would stay in deeper waters. So when Jesus took the disciples out in the boat and asked them to let their nets down they would have thought He was being ridiculous. However, they caught probably the biggest catch they'd ever caught! This shows that Jesus can do the impossible and He is in control of the fish!

Approximate Timings

9.15	Crew Countdown – Crew and Satellite Prayer Team meet together. Brief them and pray
9.45	Check-in – Security Officers give out Snonge Passports to kids and stamp the second day. Play music in the background and play Emergency Smergency while they're arriving
10.00	King Snorg's Transmission
10.05	Captain Smirk and Lieutenant Savoy welcome everyone and do a few 'Put your hands up if …'
10.15	Crew sketch
10.20	Teach the *Mission: Miracle Maker* song
10.25	Game – Musical Martians
10.40	The *Miracle Maker* video clip
11.00	Activity 1 – Making a Giant Rocket
11.20	Refreshment break
11.30	'Beam Me Up, Swotty' – Guest star: Simon Peter the disciple
11.35	Activity 2 – Split into Moonrakers and Starbusters
11.55	Captain Smirk and Lieutenant Savoy round up the day, and go through the Check-out procedure again. Distribute Homequest sheets
12.00	End of session. Crew debrief and prayer

The Miracle Maker Video Clip
Synopsis (0 hr 15 mins - 0 hr 31 mins)

Jesus begins to talk to a crowd of people. Tamar is there and she wants to stay and listen to Jesus. Jesus tells them the story of the wise and foolish builders and then He speaks to the crowds at the Sea of Galilee about faith being as small as a mustard seed. He meets the fishermen and tells them to take the boats further out and let the nets down for a catch. They think He's crazy – the fish go too deep in the daytime. But they catch so many fish that the nets begin to break. Tamar watches as Jesus talks to a room full of people. She is getting worse. Crowds gather outside the house, a paralysed man is lowered into the room. Jesus tells him to get up and forgives him of his sin. Jesus meets a distressed Mary Magdalene on the road and saves her from demons; she is a changed woman. Then we see Jesus choosing His disciples, the last one being Matthew the tax collector.

King Snorg's Transmission

Hello, everyone! King Snorg of Snonge here again. Thank you for all your hard work yesterday. The crew have reported back to me all the things that you discovered yesterday about the 'Miracle Maker'. We now know that His name is Jesus and that He was born in Bethlehem. It seems that He had a slightly unusual start in life. His mother was a lady called Mary who was engaged to a carpenter called Joseph but Joseph was not Jesus' dad. His Dad was in fact God. This seems very mysterious to us here on Snonge. Why would God send His Son to Earth to become a small helpless baby? What happened to this man Jesus? How did He cope with life on earth as a human being?

You're going to continue your investigation today and the crew have been briefed as to the information we need. They will explain to you what you're going to do.

Until tomorrow ... goodbye!

Crew Sketch

Characters: ***Captain Smirk and Lieutenant Savoy***
Props: ***packed lunch***

Captain: Wow! What a privilege to have King Snorg himself talk to us!

Lieutenant: I know. It is truly an honour.

Captain: Actually this whole mission is turning out to be quite exciting don't you think? I feel like we're on the brink of an amazing discovery.

Lieutenant: Exactly, I was so excited this morning I forgot to have my breakfast.

Captain: That's very naughty, Lieutenant. My mother says ...

Together: 'Breakfast is the most important meal of the day!'

Lieutenant: Yeah, yeah, I know. Still, I did make myself a rather yummy packed lunch.

Captain: Oh, really? What's in it, then?

Lieutenant: Well, I've got lunar fish sandwiches, a bottle of comet coke and of course a Mars bar.

Captain: All I've got is a packet of Starburst!

Lieutenant: Well, you could share my lunch if you want.

Captain: Thanks for the offer but I'm not really a lunar fish fan. In fact I just don't like fish in general.

Lieutenant: Really? Oh, I love fish.

Captain: I did used to go fishing, though. Mind you, I was pretty rubbish, and I never caught a thing! ... Except a cold, that is!

Lieutenant: Aatchoo!

Captain: Bless you!

Lieutenant: Thanks.

Captain: That's quite all right. Anyway, we'd better get back to work.

Lieutenant: Can we sing the *Mission: Miracle Maker* song first, though?

Captain: OK, but maybe we need to teach it to them today.

Game

Musical Martians

You will need: music – either CDs or your band could play.

As with Day 1, we take a well-known party game, change it slightly and give it a space name! Based on the game 'Musical Statues', music is played and everyone has to dance around. When the music stops everyone has to pretend to be a Martian and stay still. You could give them an idea of how to do this; maybe show them two or three Martian poses they can choose from. The last person to get into their Martian pose is out of the game. You keep playing this until you are left with one (or two) who are the winners.

Activity 1

Giant Rocket

You will need: five sheets of A1 white paper joined together with rocket outline on, paints, scissors, pens/crayons, brushes **(master on p.31, or as pdf on CD)**

On the opposite page is a picture of a rocket, which you will need to copy onto a large area of paper (we suggest five sheets of A1 paper arranged as shown). Once you've done this you will need to split the whole picture up into smaller sections, which you will give to the children to paint and decorate.

It's best to give small groups of children a section to decorate and have at least one leader supervising each group. On the picture you will need to write in on the sections what colour all the different parts are supposed to be so the children will know which colours go where. This will also ensure that you don't end up with a multi-coloured rocket! You could give them tin foil or milk bottle tops to decorate the rocket and give that space-type feel.

When it's all dry you can put the sections together and make one big space rocket, which you can then display in Porthole 2 for the rest of the week.

Activity 2

Starbusters

You will need: four pictures (ice-cream, sun, snowman and snow falling, bucket, spade and sandcastle: you can draw your own, or cut them out of a magazine) and a Starbusters Worksheet for each child **(worksheet master on p. 32, or as pdf on CD)**.

Have the set of four pictures ready to show them. One is a picture of an ice-cream, another a picture of the sun, another is a picture of a snowman and snow falling and the last one is a picture of a bucket, spade and a sandcastle. Then begin to talk to them about summer. Ask them which of the four pictures isn't to do with summer; get them to show you. Obviously the snow picture is the odd one out. Then get them to think what it would be like if it snowed in summer. Recap on the story of the catch of fish and explain that at that time of day you would never catch fish – a bit like snow in the summer, it would have to be a miracle! Then give them all a copy of the picture of Jesus in the boat with His disciples for them to colour in.

Moonrakers

You will need: Moonrakers Worksheet for each child **(master on p. 32, or as pdf on CD)**

Ask them how they would feel if this summer it snowed! What would they think? Does it ever happen? What do they think people would do? Ask them if they've ever seen the film *Dumbo*. Everyone laughs at Dumbo because of his big ears and no one believes he can fly because elephants don't fly! But in the story Dumbo does learn to fly – he does the impossible. Explain that when Jesus asked the disciples to try to catch fish in the middle of the day it was a ridiculous request. People don't go fishing at that time of day because you don't catch fish then! But Jesus helped them to catch a massive catch of fish – He did the impossible. So, if we had snow in the summer that would be a miracle, just as an elephant flying would be a miracle and just as catching hundreds of fish in the middle of the day would be a miracle.

Give them all a picture of Jesus, the disciples and lots of hidden fish and get them to count how many fish there are hidden in the picture. (There are 20 in total.)

Activity 1

Giant Rocket Picture

Here is an outline of the giant rocket picture for you to copy. Marked on it are the lines to split it into five sections, as well as a suggestion for the colour coding for each section.

1. Silver/grey/gold/bronze
2. Black or dark blue
3. Red
4. Purple
5. Orange
6. Cotton wool or tissue

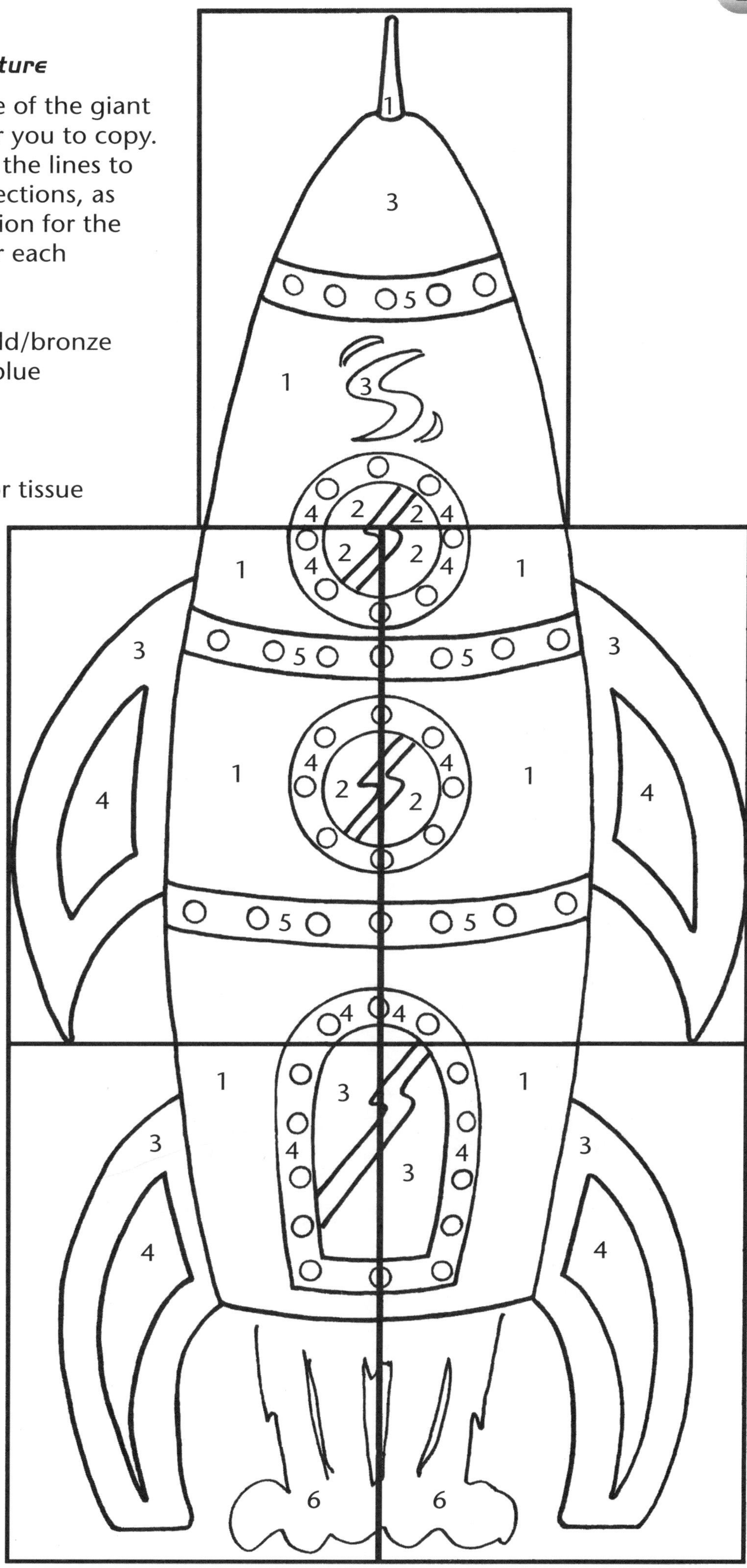

Activity 2 – Starbusters Worksheet

Here's a picture of Jesus and the disciples in the boat for you to colour in.

Moonrakers Worksheet

How many fish can you find in this picture? This is what they look like 

Beam Me Up, Swotty

While the children are having their refreshment break, Simon Peter positions himself on the beam spot. The Siren goes off and the space cadets shout 'Laser beam!' so that the children sit around the beam spot. As the jingle plays, Swotty appears.

Swotty: Hello and welcome to 'Beam Me Up, Swotty' – sponsored by Comet Cola, the drink that makes you go … *(Swotty waits for the kids to say 'PING' – if they don't he mimes it. If they don't respond the first time then he repeats the first sequence)* The show where we beam up special people from other planets. In case you weren't watching yesterday, we had an interesting chat with a woman called Mary from Israel around AD 30. She's from Planet Earth, where all this week's Beamers are from. Mary told us all about how she and her husband had a few visits from some angels and she had a son who was the Son of God, an amazing story. So again I don't know who our Beamer will be, all I know is that they're human, they will be from Israel around AD 30, and that Private SnugglePuss the Third chose them to come on the show. So let's get on with it. Do you remember how we beamed up Mary yesterday? I said something and then you said something back. Let's see if you can remember. 'Starbusters, Moonrakers, what are we waiting for?' *(Wait for kids to reply – you will probably need to mouth the words, 'Swotty, we're ready, who are we waiting for?' – if they don't say it very loudly tell them you don't think that will have worked and to try again, if successful, Simon Peter slowly starts to move – speaking to Simon Peter)* Hello, welcome to my show, 'Beam Me Up, Swotty' – sponsored by Comet Cola, the drink that makes you go *(wait for the kids to say 'PING')*. Could you please tell us your name and where you're from.

Simon Peter: Well, I'm from Israel, I used to be called Simon but now I'm called Peter.

Swotty: Right … How is that, then? Did you get bored with the name of 'Simon'?

Simon Peter: No, it changed just after I met Jesus.

Swotty: Ah now, Jesus – is that the same Jesus whose mum was Mary and who's Dad was God?

Simon Peter: Yes, the same.

Swotty: Just to check, did He have a human dad called Joseph who was a carpenter?

Simon Peter: That's correct.

Swotty: And was He born in an animal shed even though He was a king?

Simon Peter: Yes He was, and yes He is!

Swotty: I think it's probably the same one then. Did you know Him well? How did you meet Him?

Simon Peter: I was in the harbour – I'm a fisherman y'see – and everyone was talking about this new man. I thought they were all crazy! They said He would save us … then when I met Him I thought He was crazy. But then He began to talk to us. He talked for hours and we just listened. He told me and my friends to push our boat out deeper to catch some fish. Then I really thought He was mad!

Swotty: Why did that make you think He was crazy?

Simon Peter: No one catches fish during the day because the fish hide deep down in the water. We thought we'd be there for ever waiting to catch some fish! But then we brought the nets up and there were so many fish in them that the nets began to break and the fish were falling out of the boat. It was amazing!

Swotty: Had you been a fisherman long?

Simon Peter: I was brought up on fishing.

Swotty: So you know your stuff then.

Simon Peter: Yes, we all fish for a living.

Swotty: So was Jesus a fisherman? How come He knew to take the boat further out and to put the nets in the water?

Simon Peter: No, He was a carpenter and a preacher. He knew because … well, I don't know but … He told us to do it and it was the biggest catch I've ever seen!

Swotty: So would you say that it was a miracle?

Simon Peter: Definitely, and I saw many more after that.

Swotty: Well, we'd love to hear more about that Simon, I mean Peter, Simon Peter *(Swotty gets confused)* but we don't have much time left *(puts his finger in his ear as if listening to his earpiece)*. Yes, I'm just hearing now that we only have a few satellite-seconds left. So before you go, can you tell me very briefly what happened to you after the big catch and why you changed your name?

Simon Peter: Well, Jesus asked me to follow Him. So I did and I still do. He started to call me Peter because it means 'rock'. It is steady, and He said He was going to use me …

Swotty: I'm going to have to stop you there, I'm afraid. Thank you so much for coming on the show. Sum-up time then … Today our Beamer has been Simon … Peter who is from Israel 'around AD 30'. Simon Peter knew Jesus, who was the Son of God – even the fish did what He said – it truly was a miracle! Thank you to my wonderful audience today – I hope you'll join me tomorrow. And thank you to Simon Peter. Let's give him a big round of applause to beam him back to Earth.

(As the audience claps, Simon Peter waves on the spot and slowly begins to freeze. The jingle plays, Swotty waves goodbye to the audience and goes off. Do a couple of Emergency Smergencies before moving into Activity 2, during which Simon Peter disappears.)

M:MM Homequest

So here we are, Day 2, and it's time for our Homequest already. We hope you enjoyed yesterday's puzzles. Today we're going to ask John and his dog Gruff to lead us through what we're going to do; they're the next members of the Topz Gang. Take it away, guys!

Hello there! John here, and this is my dog, Gruff.I've got a twin sister called Sarah and I love to cook. I enjoy taking Gruff for a walk. He's a great friend.

OK. The first thing you need to try and do is remember the miracle that we looked at today in **Mission: Miracle Maker**. *It's written below but all the letters have been jumbled up. Can you unjumble them?*

ussJe pedleh eth ssipliced thacc dasol fo sifh

It's quite good that they asked me to help you today as it's all about fish and I love going fishing. Plus I can play a pretty good TUNA on my tambourine ... geddit? Sorry! My jokes aren't that great! Dave told me that yesterday you all learned a bit from the Bible so here's another one for you to try and learn off by heart. It's from today's story.

'They caught such a large number of fish that their nets began to break.'

Here's a puzzle for you to do. All you have to do is join the dots up and you'll find out what the hidden picture is. Have fun!

OK, folks. We're gonna have to say goodbye for now. Say goodbye, Gruff.

Benny's Joke

Where do little fishes go every morning?

What fish goes across the sea at 100mph?

Jesus heals!

Aim of Today's Session
(Mark 5: 21 - 43)

Today we'll be focusing on the healing of the woman with internal bleeding (we'll be calling her Tabitha later!). She has been very sick for a long time and the doctors can't cure her. There is no need to explain the cause of the bleeding. The emphasis is on Jesus' power to heal the sick and the lady's faith.

Approximate Timings

9.15	Crew Countdown – Crew and Satellite Prayer Team meet together. Brief them and pray
9.45	Check-in – Security Officers give out Snonge Passports to kids and stamp the third day. Play background music. Play Emergency Smergency or Musical Martians as the kids arrive
10.00	King Snorg's Transmission
10.05	Captain Smirk welcomes everyone and does a few 'Put your hands up if ...'
10.15	Crew sketch
10.20	Sing the *Mission: Miracle Maker* song
10.25	Game – Space Hopping
10.40	*The Miracle Maker* video clip
11.00	Activity 1 – Making Space Mobiles
11.20	Refreshment break
11.30	'Beam Me Up, Swotty' – Guest star: Tabitha
11.35	Split into Moonrakers and Starbusters for Activity 2
11.55	Captain Smirk and Lieutenant Savoy round up the day, and go through the Check-out procedure again
12.00	End of session. Crew debrief and prayer

Miracle Maker Video Clip
Synopsis (0hr 31 mins - 0 hr 47 mins)

Jairus' wife insists that he takes Tamar to Jesus. Jairus is not sure that he trusts Jesus. They decide to invite Jesus and His disciples for a meal to question Him. Mary Magdalene comes and washes Jesus' feet and covers them with expensive perfume. They are shocked that He would let her. Tamar is getting worse and Jairus decides to find Jesus. He believes Jesus will heal her. On the way to the house a woman is healed of internal bleeding by just touching His cloak. Jesus tells Tamar to get up and she is raised from the dead. We then see the authorities worrying about what to do with Jesus. Jesus takes His disciples to Jerusalem for the Passover feast. One night they sit around the fire and Jesus talks about the kingdom of heaven. A rich man asks Him how he can be saved. Jesus tells the story of the good Samaritan.

King Snorg's Transmission

Hello again! Welcome to Day 3 of our mission. So far we've been very successful so I think you can all give yourselves a pat on the back. Well, go on then, give yourselves a pat on the back! That's right, good. It now appears that our initial information about the 'Miracle Maker' is correct. He does indeed have some amazing powers. Somehow He seems even to be able to get fish to do what He wants. I've got a pet goldfish called Snappy and I've tried getting him to jump through a hoop but he just doesn't do what I tell him to do. Naughty Snappy! The thing we need to know is whether these powers of Jesus lasted or whether they were just a fluke. So today you'll be continuing to look at the life of our Miracle Maker. I look forward to hearing all about what you find. Oh, I must go and feed Snappy now. Until we meet again! Snappy, don't worry!

Crew Sketch

Characters: ***Captain Smirk and Lieutenant Savoy***

Props: ***Box of tissues***

(Lieutenant comes in with box of tissues being really melodramatic – he has a cold! He sounds really bunged up and keeps sneezing!)

Captain: Good morning, Lieutenant. How are you this fine day?

Lieutenant: Well, it's fuddy you should mention dat, Captain, but I've got a really bad cold.

Captain: Oh dear! But I guess you were sneezing a bit yesterday, weren't you?

Lieutenant: Yes … Aatchoo!

Captain: Bless you.

Lieutenant: Thank you – it's really addoying because I'm all bunged up. Aatchoo!

Captain: I know. You have my sympathy … just don't give it to me, OK!

Lieutenant: I'll try not to. Aatchoo!

Captain: Maybe you should go back to bed?

Lieutenant: Well, I would but I don't want to miss out on anything exciting.

Captain: Look, I think you need to go and rest; I'll make sure you know if anything happens.

Lieutenant: OK. If you're … Aatchoo! … sure?

Captain: I'm sure! Maybe you'll feel a bit better later today and you can join us. Do you want me to make you a honey-and-lemon drink?

Lieutenant: If you don't … Aatchoo! … mind?

Captain: No, you go and lie down, I'll just sing the *Mission: Miracle Maker* song with the crew here. Then I'll make you your drink, OK?

Lieutenant: Thank you, Captain. Sorry I'm not much … Aatchoo! … use to you today.

Captain: Don't worry about it, we can't help being ill. Now go!

Lieutenant: OK. Bye for now, everyone. Have a good day … Aatchoo! *(Goes off stage)*

Captain: Oh dear, poor Lieutenant Savoy. It's horrible being ill, isn't it! Well, I guess we don't want to waste any more time. We've got lots to do today. Let's sing our song. Take it away!

Game

Space Hopping

Get everyone to stand as a group in the middle of the room. On your instruction everyone then 'bounces' around the room saying, 'Space hopping, space hopping, bounce, bounce, bounce'. Everyone says this together following your lead. You then choose a letter of the alphabet, which you call out. Everyone then has to think of an object or animal beginning with that letter and then stop bouncing and pretend to be that thing. You then go round the group and everyone says what they are. If any two or more people have become the same object/animal they are out of the game. If you're feeling kind then you could give everyone more than one life so they don't go out straightaway.

Activity 1

Space Mobiles

For each child you will need: 2 fronts and 2 backs of Spacemen; two Card Planets; front and back of each Spaceship; 2 green garden sticks and 2 metres fishing line/string **(master on p. 40 or as pdf on CD)**.

On page 40 are outlines of spacemen/women doing space walks, a spaceship and a planet. The idea is to photocopy them, get the children to colour in the shapes, then cut out the objects to create a hanging mobile. The shapes are symmetrical so you can stick them back to back and have colour on both sides. This will also add more weight to make the mobile hang better. Once finished, leaders can cross-tie two green garden sticks, then attach the figures to the ends and middle with fishing line. These can then be hung in Porthole 3.

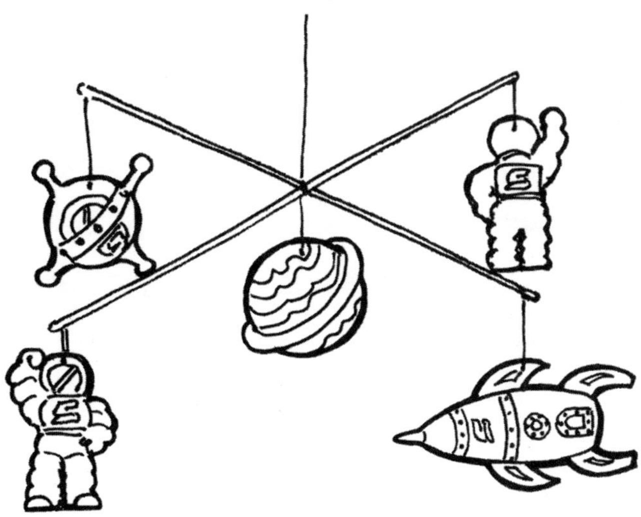

Activity 2

Starbusters

For each child you will need: A4 paper, pen/pencil

Give them all a piece of A4 paper (turned sideways to a landscape position) with a line down the middle dividing it into two A5 sections. Then get them to think about how they feel when they are poorly and then in the first section draw a picture of how they feel when they're ill. Then in the other section draw a picture of how they feel when they're better.

Then gather them around you and maybe get a couple of them to tell you about their pictures. Then recap on the story of the sick lady and how she was very ill and had been for a long time. The doctors couldn't give her any medicine to make her better. Ask the children how they think the lady's family would have felt when she was really ill. But she touched Jesus and then she was totally better! Ask the children how they think the lady's family would have felt when Jesus made her well again! Isn't that amazing. Ask them what they think the lady might have said to Jesus when she was well again! Thank you maybe?! Depending on the group and the amount of time you could maybe pray with them thanking God for what they've learned today.

Moonrakers

For each child you will need: Moonrakers Worksheet and pen/pencil for each child **(master on p. 41 or as pdf on CD)**.

Ask the group how they feel when they're ill. Discuss their answers. Then ask them how they feel when they're better. Discuss. Ask them how they think Tabitha's family felt when she got really sick. Discuss but be sensitive to the fact that someone in the group may have a family member who is ill. Ask them what Jesus did. Then ask how Tabitha's family felt after Jesus had healed her. Isn't it amazing! Give each member of the group the two pictures of Jesus with the sick lady, then get them to try and find the 10 differences between the two pictures.

Then spend a couple of minutes praying with the group, thanking God for what they've learned today.

Activity 1 – Space Mobile

Here are the pictures for the Space Mobiles.

Activity 2 - Moonrakers Worksheet

Can you spot ten differences between the two pictures of Jesus and the sick lady?

Beam Me Up, Swotty

While the children are having their refreshment break, Tabitha positions herself on the beam spot. The Siren goes off and the Captain shouts 'Laser Beam' so that the children sit around the beam spot. As the jingle plays, Swotty appears.

Swotty: Hello and welcome to 'Beam Me Up, Swotty' – sponsored by Comet Cola, the drink that … *(Swotty waits for the kids to say 'makes you go PING!')* The show where we beam up special people from other planets. Hopefully you were with us yesterday when we met Simon Peter the fisherman from Israel 'around AD 30' on the Planet Earth. Simon Peter told us about a life-changing, massive, miracle catch of fish. I never knew fish could be so interesting. My dad took me fishing once. I sat for hours trying to catch something and when I did it was only the size of my thumb *(holds up thumb)*. And my thumb was smaller then! *(puts finger in ear)* Yes, yes! *(talking to director)* OK, let's get going. You know what happens next, right? Ready? Starbusters, Moonrakers what are we waiting for? *(kids reply and Tabitha begins to move slowly)* Hello! *(whispers to the audience)* Well, I never! Our Beamer of the day is a little older than our previous guests this week. *(Turns to talk to Tabitha again)* Welcome to my show, 'Beam Me Up, Swotty' sponsored by Comet Cola, the drink that … *(wait for kids to say, 'makes you go PING')* Would you like to just introduce yourself to us?

Tabitha: Hello. My name is Tabitha.

Swotty: Well, it's very nice to meet you Tabitha. I'm presuming that you're from Israel around AD 30 on the Planet Earth.

Tabitha: Yes, I suppose so.

Swotty: You don't sound so sure!

Tabitha: Well I do live in Israel but I'm never sure of what the date is. That sounds about right, though.

Swotty: OK. So Tabitha, tell us a bit about yourself.

Tabitha: Well I've just recently started my own business. I'm so pleased. It's a been a dream of mine. I've always loved making things but I just haven't been able to do it until now.

Swotty: What exactly is the business, then?

Tabitha: I sell cloth – beautiful colours and patterns from all over the country. And we make clothes to order too.

Swotty: Sounds good … So, erm, I don't mean to be rude but, why did you leave it … so late in life?

Tabitha: Well, I got married and had children, and when they were grown up, old enough to look after themselves, I got ill.

Swotty: Oh I'm sorry to hear that. What was wrong with you?

Tabitha: Well, the doctors weren't really sure but it made me weak and tired and I was in a lot of pain.

Swotty: How long were you in pain for?

Tabitha: About twelve years! It was a long twelve years, and I was really losing hope. I had tried everything. I was running out of money because I had seen so many doctors and 'experts' but they couldn't help me.

Swotty: So what worked in the end?

Tabitha: Well, I heard about this man who was travelling around, talking to people, healing them and telling them about God. So I found out where He was and fought my way through the crowd to see Him.

Swotty: His name wasn't Jesus, was it?!

Tabitha: Yes, it was Jesus. He healed me and my life has been totally transformed!

Swotty: When you say He healed you ... what did He actually do?

Tabitha: Well, I knew He had power to do amazing things. I knew He was a busy man and I didn't want to interrupt, so I just thought that if I could just touch His cloak it would heal me.

Swotty: So did it work?

Tabitha: Yes! As I touched His cloak I felt something go through my body and I felt totally better. I knew I was healed and I haven't had any problems ever since.

Swotty: Wow! That's incredible! ... So you didn't even speak to Jesus?

Tabitha: No, but He did turn around and speak to me afterwards.

Swotty: Surely He didn't know you'd touched His cloak?

Tabitha: He stopped and said He felt power come out of Him. Then He told me that it was because I believed that I was healed. And I was and it was the best thing that has ever happened to me.

Swotty: Well, this week on 'Beam Me Up, Swotty', sponsored by Comet Cola, the drink that *(wait for the kids to reply 'makes you go PING')* we have heard some incredible stories. Tabitha, I wouldn't mind meeting this Jesus guy! Ow! *(Swotty holds his ear as if the director has shouted down the earpiece at him)* OK, OK! I'm so sorry, Tabitha. We are going to have to leave it there, our time is up. Thank you to my fantastic audience – you've been great. And thanks to our third Beamer of the week who was ill for many years, but Jesus healed her just by her touching His cloak – what a miracle! Let's give Tabitha a big round of applause to beam her back to Earth.

(As the audience claps Tabitha waves on the spot, but slowly begins to freeze. The jingle plays, Swotty waves goodbye to the audience and goes off. Do a couple of Emergency Smergencies before moving on to Activity 2, during which Tabitha disappears.)

M:MM Homequest

Now it's time to try and learn another bit from the Bible. Can you remember the other bits you've already learned? Well, here's today's sentence …

'Your faith has healed you.'

It's Homequest time again, folks. We hope you've had fun today at *Mission: Miracle Maker*. Today we're going to meet Josie. So here she is!

Hi everyone! Yep, I'm Josie. I gather you met John and Gruff yesterday; you'll meet some of the others later. Anyway, what can I tell you about myself? Well, I live in a block of flats. We're on the top floor so it's just as well I'm not afraid of heights! At school I really like PE and I also play the violin … I feel sorry for my neighbours sometimes! Anyway let's get on with the Homequest. First, can you remember what today's miracle was? It's written below but it's been written in the Topz code so you'll need to use the Topz codesheet to help you crack the code.

It's really cool being a Christian because you have God with you all the time, even when you're frightened or feeling sad. The lady must have been so pleased that Jesus healed her! Here's a picture of her for you to colour in.

We're close to the end of today's Homequest. Just Benny's joke to make you groan now! Bye!

Benny's Joke

What illness did everyone catch on the Starship Enterprise?

Jesus raises people from the dead!

Aim of Today's Session (John 11:1 – 44)

Today we'll be focusing on the raising of Lazarus from the dead. Yesterday we looked at how Jesus healed the sick lady. The fact that Jesus was able to bring Lazarus back to life even though he had been buried for a few days shows that Jesus really does have power over death. We'll be looking a bit at how we feel when people die, how sad it is and then explaining how exciting it is that Jesus has the power to bring people back to life.

Approximate Timings

9.15	Crew Countdown – Crew and Satellite Prayer Team meet together. Brief them and pray
9.45	Check-in – Security Officers give out Snonge Passports to kids and stamp the fourth day. Play background music. Play 'Emergency Smergency' or 'Space Hopping' as the kids arrive
10.00	King Snorg's Transmission
10.05	Captain Smirk welcomes everyone and does a few 'Put your hands up if …'
10.15	Crew Sketch
10.20	Sing the *Mission: Miracle Maker* song
10.25	Game – Stuck in the Vortex
10.40	*The Miracle Maker* video clip
11.00	Activity 1 – Making Planets
11.20	Refreshment Break
11.30	'Beam Me Up, Swotty' – Guest star: Lazarus
11.35	Split into Moonrakers and Starbusters for Activity 2
11.55	Captain Smirk and Lieutenant Savoy round up the day and the kids check out
12.00	End of session. Crew debrief and prayer

Miracle Maker Video Clip Synopsis (0 hr 47 mins – 1 hr 07 mins)

Jesus stands with Tamar looking over the countryside. Reuben rushes to tell Jesus of Lazarus' severe illness, passing on Mary and Martha's request for Him to go. Jesus replies that He will go, but not just yet. The high priest Caiaphas is told of Jesus' visit to Lazarus' tomb. Jesus tells them to take away the stone and orders the dead man to come out. He tells Lazarus' sisters to remove the bandages from Lazarus. The crowds believe in Jesus and follow Him to Jerusalem. Arriving at the synagogue, Jesus is angry that it has been turned into a market place. Religious leaders quiz Jesus about Caesar's taxes. Judas disagrees with Jesus and doubts He is their Saviour. Judas tells the Romans he will take them to Jesus. Jesus and the disciples eat a meal together (the Last Supper). Jesus goes alone to pray. When He returns, Judas brings the Roman soldiers to arrest Jesus and take Him to the high priest. As Jesus had foretold, Simon Peter denies he knows Jesus three times. On the third time, the cockerel crows, and Jesus walks past a weeping Simon Peter.

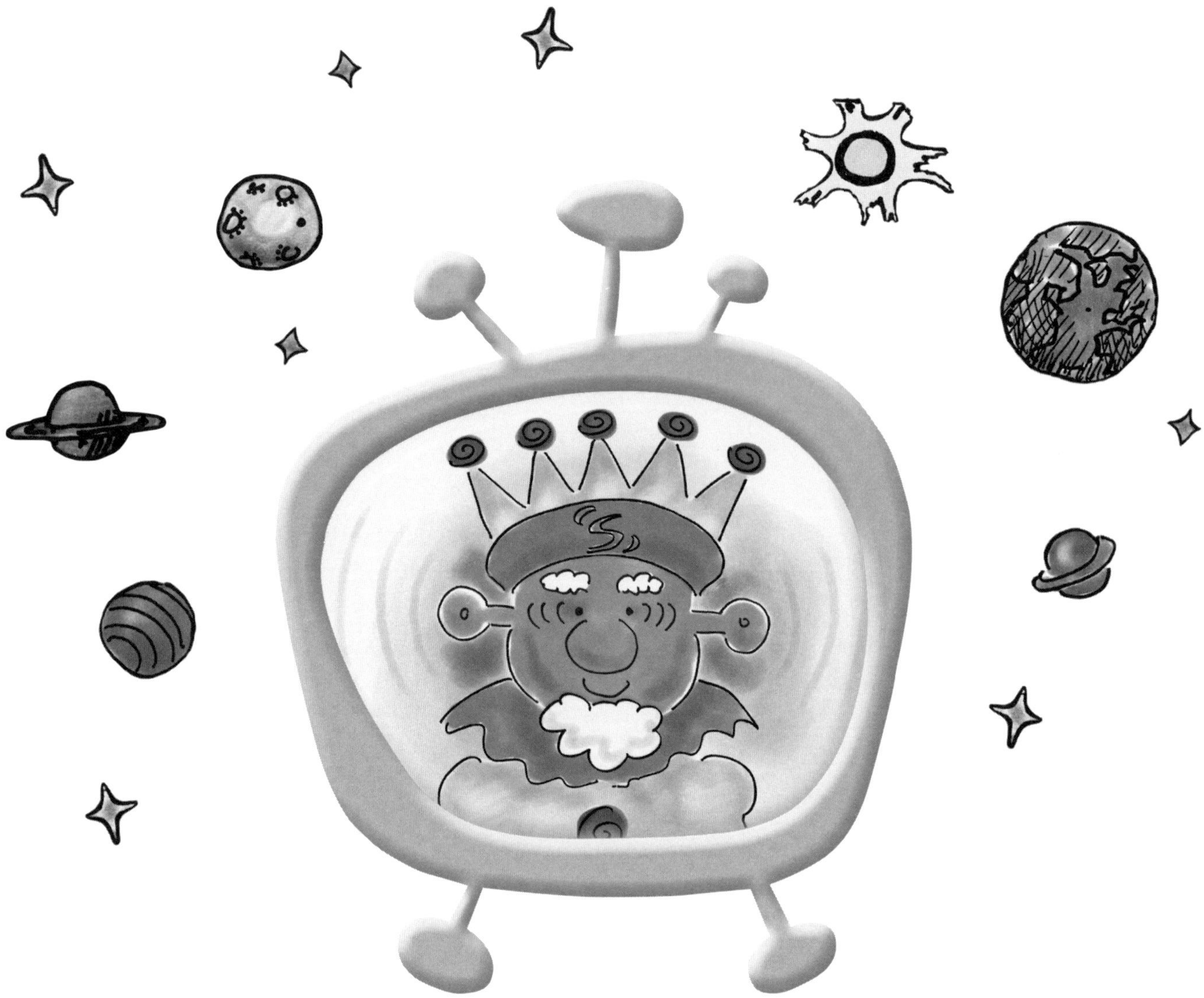

King Snorg's Transmission

Hello again! I don't know about you but I've been really enjoying finding out about Jesus, the Miracle Maker. He is obviously a remarkable person. I can't believe we didn't hear about Him before. You'd think the whole world would want to know about a man who is actually God and who can not only produce a massive catch of fish out of nowhere but can also heal a woman who even the best doctors can't help. It's amazing! You human beings are full of surprises! Still, it's good that we're finding out about Him now. The big question today is, 'What will He do next?' I guess that's my cue, then, to hand back to the crew so thank you all again. Until tomorrow ... Goodbye!

Crew Sketch

Characters: ***Captain Smirk and Lieutenant Savoy***
Props: ***matchbox***

(Captain comes in looking very sad, carrying a matchbox very carefully in his hand.)

Lieutenant: Good morning, Captain. Thanks for letting me take it easy yesterday, I feel a whole lot better today. *(Notices that Captain is sad)* How are you?
Captain: Well, to tell you the truth, Lieutenant – and this is slightly embarrassing – I'm a bit upset today.
Lieutenant: Oh dear! Why? What's happened?
Captain: Well, now, I might start crying as I tell you ... you see ...*(sniff, sniff)* ... You know my pet ladybird, Penelope?
Lieutenant: Yes, the one that flew in through the airlock the other day?
Captain: That's right, and you know how much I cared for her ... I made her a nice home, talked to her a lot and I even showed her my stamp collection.
Lieutenant: Oh yes. I hope she understands that you only show your best friends your stamp collection, and that matchbox you picked for her was one of the finest matchboxes I've ever seen.
Captain: I know, I know. I even wrote her name in the side *(starts to cry a bit)*
Lieutenant: Yeah, I'm sure all the other insects are bored and are all jealous of Penelope's pad.
Captain: But that's just it, you see ... they can't be anymore ... because she's gone!
Lieutenant: Gone? Gone where?
Captain: *(getting more and more upset)* To meet her maker *(starts crying)*
Lieutenant: Oh, that'll be nice. Like a little reunion. I'm sure she'll appreciate it.
Captain: No, you don't understand. She's gone to the big ladybird in the sky!
Lieutenant: Well, she probably hadn't seen her mum for a while. It's important to spend time ...
Captain: No, no, no. She's kicked the bucket.
Lieutenant: What, that tiny little thing? However did she manage ...?
Captain: No, no, no! She's GONE TO SLEEP FOREVER!
Lieutenant: Wow! She must be tired, and anyway I thought she'd gone to see her mum?
Captain: LOOK! Lieutenant, I don't think you understand. SHE DIED!
Lieutenant: OK, OK. There's no need to shout about it ... Shouldn't you show more respect for the dead?
Captain: Exactly! That's why I'm feeling so sad. My little Penelope died.
Lieutenant: Oh, Captain. I'm so sorry. How stupid and insensitive of me. I understand now. Do you know why she died?
Captain: Well, I think maybe she wasn't meant to be put into a little matchbox and I spoke to the ship's doctor and ... Well, how was I supposed to know ladybirds don't eat chocolate? *(gets very upset now)* It's all my fault.
Lieutenant: Now calm down, calm down, Captain. It wasn't your fault. You just didn't know, that's all. We've never had a ladybird on board. How were we supposed to know?
Captain: Well, I hadn't thought of it like that.
Lieutenant: You tried your best to look after her and that's what really matters.
Captain: Really ...? You think so ...? I guess I did.
Lieutenant: Of course you did.
Captain: Oh, thank you, Lieutenant. I feel a lot better now.
Lieutenant: Good. I'm glad. Now I know what will cheer you up.
Captain: What?
Lieutenant: Let's all sing the *Mission: Miracle Maker* song.
Captain: What a great idea!

Game

Stuck in the Vortex

Once again this is based on a game you're probably familiar with. Choose one person from the group. They are going to be 'Zing the Zong'. Everyone else is a Snonge space cadet and they have to start running around the room. On your instruction Zing the Zong is released into the group and has to trap the space cadets by touching them either on the arm or back. As soon as a space cadet is trapped by Zing the Zong, they have to stand still with their arms out at their sides. They have to stay like that until another space cadet sets them free by going under each arm in turn and saying 'Snonge'. They are then free to join in the game again. If you want to, you could get someone to become another Zing the Zong so you have two trying to trap the space cadets.

Activity 1

Creating Space

You will need: Lots of planet stencils **(masters on p. 49, or as pdf on CD)**, a large sheet of paper, paint, sponges (you could use cut up car sponges), paper plates, newspaper

Today you will be making a large picture of space using the diagrams of stencils on the opposite page. You can either copy or photocopy the plans here or make up some of your own, or both! It is best to make quite a lot of stencils to go around all the children. First put lots of newspaper on the floor so paint doesn't go everywhere! Try to get a large roll of paper (wall lining paper would be good), and lay it out over the newspaper. Write a title which says something like, 'On a Mission to Find Jesus'.

Place paper plates around the large paper for the paint to go in, and have plenty of sponge pieces; at least a couple for each plate. Get the children to dab the paint through the stencils onto the large paper to make a huge space-like scene. If there's time you could label one planet 'Snonge' and one 'Earth', then get some children to chart a course on dotted lines from one to the other. At the end of the activity, pray with the children, thanking God for sending Jesus to live on earth.

Activity 2

Starbusters

You will need: 2 Starbusters Worksheets for each child, cut out stones (two per child), glue, pens and pencils **(masters on p. 49, or as pdf on CD)**.

Recap on today's Crew Sketch where Captain Smirk's pet ladybird died. Ask the children if they've had a pet that died. How did they feel? Explain that death is not a nice thing. We get very sad when our pets die but it's even sadder when people we know die. Recap on the story of Lazarus. He'd died and his friends and family were really upset, especially his two sisters. Jesus was able to bring him back to life, even after he'd been buried. Isn't that amazing? Get them to do a before and after picture using the picture on the opposite page. You will need to photocopy it so they each have two copies of the picture on one page. They will need to stick the stone which covers the entrance to the tomb in the right place on each picture, i.e. while Lazarus was in the tomb the stone covered the entrance then it was moved away. They will need to draw Lazarus in the second picture and also draw in people's faces in both pictures, i.e. sad faces when Lazarus was dead then happy when he was raised from the dead.

Spend a few minutes praying, perhaps ask if any of the children know someone who is ill, then you could pray for them.

Moonrakers

You will need: Moonrakers Worksheet for each child **(master on p. 50, or as pdf on CD)**, pens and pencils

Recap on the story of Lazarus, asking key questions so as to jog their memories. Particularly draw out the point that the people who knew Lazarus were very sad when he died. Then give them all a copy of the *Daily Donkey* front page and explain that they need to write a short summary of the story of Lazarus for the newspaper and they need to write it in the column provided, under the heading 'Lazarus is Alive!'. They also need to draw a picture in the box provided.

Spend a few minutes praying with the group. Ask them if anyone knows someone who is ill, then you could pray for them.

Activity 1 – Creating Space

Here are the planet stencils. You need to enlarge them to create a good-sized picture, and if possible copy them onto card.

Activity 2

Starbusters Worksheet

OK, folks, you need to complete two pictures: one before Lazarus was raised from the dead and one after. Can you put the stone that goes over the entrance to the tomb in the right place on each picture? Now draw in the faces of the people who were there – were they happy or sad? Lastly you need to draw Lazarus on the after picture. If you've got time you could start colouring them in.

Activity 2 - Moonrakers Worksheet

The Daily Donkey

Price:
5 shekels

Your news brought clippety clop to you!

Lazarus is Alive!

Beam Me Up, Swotty

While the children are having their refreshment break, Lazarus positions himself on the beam spot. The Siren goes off and the Captain and Lieutenant shout 'Laser beam!' so that the children sit around the beam spot. As the jingle plays, Swotty appears.

Swotty: Hello and welcome to 'Beam Me Up, Swotty' – sponsored by Comet Cola, the drink that makes you go … *(Swotty waits for the kids to go 'PING')* The show where we beam up special people from other planets. We really have been meeting some space-tastic people this week and hearing out-of-this-universe stories. Tabitha, who spoke to us yesterday, I'm told, was the oldest Beamer that we've ever had on the show. We're going to check if she can go in the *Gravity Book of Records*. Tabitha was telling us about how a man called Jesus healed her when she was really sick. I tell you what – if you've missed a show this week, you really have missed out! So who wants to get on and see who Private SnugglePuss the Third is beaming over to us today? *(Wait for kids to reply)* OK, you lot should know the deal by now. Are you ready? *(Wait for kids to reply)* Starbusters, Moonrakers, what are we waiting for? *(Kids reply, 'Swotty, we're ready, who are we waiting for?')* And Lazarus begins to move. Hello and welcome, Sir, to 'Beam me up, Swotty', sponsored by Comet Cola, the drink … *(Wait for kids to finish sentence)* How are you doing?

Lazarus: Erm … Good I think

Swotty: It's a strange feeling isn't it? Being beamed. We're thinking of doing a new series soon where I get beamed to other planets instead of the other way round – but I'm not sure I fancy it … Anyway, I'm so sorry, I haven't properly introduced myself. I am Swotty – this is my show. Could you please tell people who you are and where you come from?

Lazarus: Certainly, my name is Lazarus and I am from Israel.

Swotty: Yes, I guess I already knew you'd be from Israel – sorry. Can you tell us a little about yourself, Lazarus? I'm sure you're a nice guy but I'm not sure you'll be able to match up to the things we've been hearing about so far this week!

Lazarus: Who have you met then, anyone I know?

Swotty: Well, we met a lady called Mary, who was the mother of Jesus; a man called Simon Peter who did what Jesus told him, and caught a whole bunch of fish, *and* – this is even more amazing – a lady called Tabitha who was seriously ill and was healed by – yep, you guessed it – Jesus. I don't suppose, by any chance, you know Him?

Lazarus: Oh yes, very well actually. My sisters and I are good friends with Him and in fact are forever in debt to Him because I actually died and He brought me back to life!!!

Swotty: What!?! You mean you were really ill and He healed you, right?

Lazarus: No, no. I was properly dead.

Swotty: Properly? What do you mean by that?

Lazarus: Well, my sisters had wrapped my body in cloth and special oils and put me in a tomb. Jesus didn't arrive till I'd already been dead for four days!

Swotty: Four days?!? Don't bodies start to smell a bit after a while?

Lazarus: Yep! I stank!

Swotty: So what happened then? Why didn't Jesus heal you before you died?

Lazarus: Well I had got really ill and my sisters sent for Jesus but He didn't come. No one could really understand why. Anyway the illness eventually got too much and I died. My sisters and my friends were really upset that Jesus had not come. When He arrived He told them to take away the stone that covered my tomb. My sister told Him that it would smell but He was pretty definite about it. He told them that if they believed then they would see how amazing God is, so they took away the stone and Jesus told me to come out. I remember hearing Him call my name and taking my hand. He helped me get up and He took me outside, then my sisters took the cloths off so that I could see ...

Swotty: Hang on ... so Jesus just called your name and told you to get up and you'd been dead for four days?

Lazarus: Yes, I was dead and Jesus made me alive again!

Swotty: Man, that is a miracle of truly universal proportions! So it was just you, your sisters and Jesus?

Lazarus: Oh, no! There were loads of people around. They were all quite shocked, although some people thought Jesus was a magician and that it was all just a trick.

Swotty: OK, thank you, Lazarus. I didn't think you could do it but you've managed to keep up the standard again today. I would ask how your experience changed your life – but I guess that's obvious! *(Listens in his earpiece)* No, is it really? *(Speaking to Lazarus again)* Our time is up, I'm afraid, Lazarus. I'd love to get you back on the show some time. Anyway thank you once again to my audience and of course to my Beamer of the day, Lazarus, who was dead, but Jesus brought him back to life again! If I was you I would cancel any plans you have tomorrow so that you don't miss the last show of the week. I'm sure it will be a corker. Until then, take care. Let's give Lazarus a big round of applause on his way back to Earth.

(As they clap, Lazarus waves on the spot but slowly begins to freeze. The jingle plays and Swotty waves goodbye to the audience and goes off. Do a couple of Emergency Smergencies before moving into Activity 2. While you're doing this Lazarus disappears.)

M:MM Homequest

Here we are again, ready to do our Homequest. Today we're going to meet Sarah from the Topz Gang, so I'll let her introduce herself.

Hi boys and girls, how are you? You've already met my twin brother John and our dog Gruff so I don't need to say much about them. I've got a cat called Saucy who is really sweet. I go to school with Josie, she and I are really good friends. I enjoy singing and playing the keyboard and like doing crafty things like painting and drawing. I hope you've enjoyed your time on the ***Millennium Parrot*** *so far, it looks like great fun. The question is, can you remember what today's miracle was? It's been written backwards again so get your mirrors at the ready!*

Jesus raised Lazarus from the dead!

Now I've seen some pretty amazing things before but I've never seen anyone raised from the dead. Imagine what it must have been like to be there! Anyway, it's time now to try and learn another little bit from the Bible. It's from today's story. See how you get on.

Jesus said: 'Whoever lives and believes in me will never die.'

Wow, what a promise! If we know God we can live with Him forever! Well, I guess it's time for another little puzzle now. Look at the picture and colour in the shapes that have a dot in. Then see what it says.

Did you get that OK? Well, it's been great meeting you all, I hope you've enjoyed today's Homequest. Here's Benny's joke – and I think it might be about my cat Saucy! Bye – see you tomorrow.

Benny's Joke

What happened to the cat who swallowed a ball of wool?

And here's one about my favourite subject – food! What two things can't you eat for breakfast?

DAY 5

Jesus is still alive!

Aim of Today's Session
(Matthew 28:1 - 20)

Today we will be looking at the miracle of Jesus' resurrection. This is the climax to the whole video, so make a big deal of it! By the end of today the children should understand that although Jesus died He didn't stay dead and He's still alive today. He wants us all to know Him and enjoy life with Him. This is the heart of the Christian message and is what we want them all to go away from this club knowing!

Approximate Timings

9.15	Crew Countdown – Crew and Satellite Prayer Team meet together. Brief them and pray
9.45	Check-in – Security Officers give out Snonge Passports to kids and stamp the fifth day. Play background music and play Emergency Smergency or Stuck in the Vortex
10.00	King Snorg's Transmission
10.05	Captain Smirk and Lieutenant Savoy welcome everyone and do a few 'Put your hand up if …'
10.15	Crew Sketch
10.20	Sing the *Mission: Miracle Maker* song
10.25	Game – Snorg Says
10.40	*The Miracle Maker* video clip
11.00	Activity 1 – Space Badges
11.20	Refreshment Break
11.30	'Beam Me Up, Swotty' – Guest star: Mary Magdalene
11.35	Activity 2 – Split into Moonrakers and Starbusters
11.55	Captain Smirk and Lieutenant Savoy round up the day and summarise the week. Thank everyone. If you have follow-up sessions planned, explain how they can be involved. Give out invites. Invite the parents/guardians in and get the children to sing the *Mission: Miracle Maker* song. Let the children show their parents/guardians the artwork they've made; they can then take it home
12.00	End of session. Crew debrief and prayer

The Miracle Maker Video Clip
Synopsis (1 hr 7 mins - 1 hr 25 mins)

Jesus' claim to be the Christ is brought to Pilate by the high priest. Jesus remains silent when charged, and is sent to Herod for trial. Herod dresses Jesus in robes and a crown of thorns, then sends Him back to Pilate. Pilate announces to the people that Jesus is innocent, asking them to choose between Barabbas and Jesus. Jesus carries His wooden cross through the streets to His crucifixion. His disciples and friends watch in desperation and disbelief. Religious leaders question His claim to be the Son of God, telling Him to come down if it is true. As Jesus takes His last breath, the Temple curtain is torn in two. Jesus' body is taken to the tomb. Mary Magdalene grieves: on returning to the tomb, she finds it empty. Jesus appears to her. Calling her by name, she realises it is Jesus. He tells her to go and tell everyone He is back. As Peter is sceptical, Mary takes him back to the empty tomb. Thomas is disbelieving – until Jesus appears to him too. We then see Jesus talking to crowds on a hilltop. He tells them to make disciples of all nations and that the Holy Spirit is coming. Jesus disappears. Tamar comforts a distressed child, telling them not to worry because 'He is with us forever'.

King Snorg's Transmission

Welcome back, intrepid space explorers! This is the last broadcast I'll be making to you from Snonge. On behalf of all the crew and citizens of Snonge I would like to thank you once again for all your hard work over the last few days. We have nearly all the information we need about the Miracle Maker Jesus. It seems that He really can raise people from the dead. However, there's just one piece of the jigsaw left to find and then our mission will be complete. That's your task for today: to gather the final piece of information. I know you can do it.

Don't forget, if you're ever passing Snonge, you can always fly in for a visit. Me and Snappy, my goldfish, would love to see you and welcome you to our planet. So without further ado I'll say farewell. Thank you again. This is King Snorg of Snonge signing off.

Crew Sketch

Characters: ***Captain Smirk and Lieutenant Savoy***
Props: ***empty glass bottle with tomato ketchup label***

(Captain comes on and notices empty tomato ketchup bottle on the floor)

Captain: Oh! Who's been leaving their rubbish around? *(Lieutenant comes in, scratching his head)*
Lieutenant: *(comes on muttering)* Now if the chicken comes first, that would mean the egg had to be created after, but how did the chicken get there if …
Captain: Are you all right, Lieutenant? You seem a bit confused.
Lieutenant: Oh, Captain, sorry, I didn't see you there.
Captain: That's all right. What seems to be the problem?
Lieutenant: Well, I've just been wondering about which came first, the chicken or the egg?
Captain: Ah, yes, the good old chicken-and-egg puzzle. Have you come up with an answer?
Lieutenant: No, not really, but I'll tell you something. All this talk about eggs has made me hungry! I really fancy a fried egg sandwich.
Captain: Oh, yes! Now you mention it, that does sound like a good idea. Mind you, someone has obviously used up all the ketchup *(hold up bottle)* so we'd have to go without it.
Lieutenant: Well, I'm more of a brown sauce fan myself anyway.
Captain: I guess I'll have to throw this away, then. Why can't people just clear up after themselves …?
Lieutenant: Hang on, Captain. Don't throw it away.
Captain: What?
Lieutenant: Well, it's glass, so we can recycle it.
Captain: Oh yeah. Silly me, I forgot. What a good idea.
Lieutenant: I only remember because my mum always got us to recycle things, she's good like that.
Captain: Mmm … I wonder who came up with the idea of recycling? It's amazing that they can take old rubbish and make it into something new.
Lieutenant: I know. That ketchup bottle could once have been a jam jar!
Captain: *(chuckles)* Yes! You know what, it's a bit like an egg really.
Lieutenant: Eh? You what?!
Captain: Well, it's all to do with new life, isn't it!
Lieutenant: I'm sorry, Captain, I don't quite follow …
Captain: Well, the egg that a chicken lays contains new life – a baby chick.
Lieutenant: Yeah, I follow that … But what's that got to do with jam jars?
Captain: Well, when you recycle things, it's a bit like giving them new life, you're making something new.
Lieutenant: Oh yes. I'd never thought of it like that … That's amazing!
Captain: Well there you go. Who'd have thought a jam jar and an egg could have something in common?
Lieutenant: Yeah
Captain: *(Looks at watch)* Goodness! Is that the time? Lieutenant, this is the last day of our mission and we've still got lots to do so we'd better get on with it.
Lieutenant: Ah, not before we sing the *Mission: Miracle Maker* song though … Don't forget!
Captain: Of course! Silly me! I guess we'll hand over to the crew for the last time. That's quite sad actually. Still we've had lots of fun, haven't we? *(asks the children)* Haven't we?! OK let's sing!

Game

Snorg Says

As the name suggests, this game is based on the game 'Simon says'. So you need to get everyone into the middle of the room. Someone needs to be King Snorg who leads the game through. Ideally Snorg should be an adult. Snorg gives a series of commands to the group, e.g. jump up and down. However, the idea is that the players only do what Snorg says if he first says 'Snorg Says …' If he doesn't say that first they're not supposed to do it. If they get it wrong they're out of the game. Whoever is Snorg will have to be quite clever at trying to catch them out, switching quite quickly between commands starting with 'Snorg says' and ones that don't.

Activity 1

Space Badges

You will need: a badge maker (if you can get one), or cardboard, safety pins, sticky tape and sticky-backed plastic (if you can't get a badge maker), pens/pencils, badge templates (if you're using them) – **(masters on p. 58, or as pdf on CD)**

If you can get hold of a badge maker that would be great. If not then some thickish card, sticky tape, sticky-backed plastic and safety pins will do just as well. The children are going to make badges to commemorate their trip. If you do not have a special badge maker then give each child a small piece of card big enough for them to draw a circle from the bottom of a tea mug on. Into this circle they can make a design of their choice to commemorate their week or you could use the designs on the next page, which they can colour in. Ideas might be: the words, 'I'VE BEEN ON THE *MILLENNIUM PARROT*', or 'I'VE BEEN ON *MISSION: MIRACLE MAKER*'. Once the designs have been drawn, the circles can be cut out, covered in sticky-backed plastic, then a safety pin stuck to the back with sticky tape. The space travellers can then take their memento home!

Activity 2

By the end of this activity you should be able to make a display that looks something like the example on p. 59

Starbusters

You will need: a picture of a butterfly, outlines of letters to spell 'Thank you Jesus for new life!', felt pens/paint/crayons.

Have a picture of a butterfly to show them. Ask them if they know how a butterfly gets to be a butterfly. Then explain how a butterfly starts off as a caterpillar – it's very small and not very beautiful! Then the caterpillar becomes a chrysalis for a while. It's almost as if the caterpillar has died. But then, one day the chrysalis comes open and out pops a beautiful butterfly! When Jesus died it was really upsetting for all his friends and family. They thought it had all come to an end. Just like when a caterpillar becomes a chrysalis, it looks like it's the end for the caterpillar. Jesus was buried and everyone was sad. But three days later Jesus came back to life. Just like the butterfly comes out of the chrysalis. Jesus didn't stay dead and He's alive today, just like He was then. He wants to be our Friend and for us to enjoy life with Him. Let's say thank you to Jesus by colouring in the letters and displaying them on the wall in the fifth porthole. The letters spell THANK YOU JESUS FOR NEW LIFE!

Pray with them that they will know Jesus as their Friend.

Moonrakers

You will need: outlines of letters that make words 'love, peace, hope, joy', outlines of the pictures to go with these words, felt pens/paints/crayons **(example on p. 59)**

Ask whether anyone has ever found a caterpillar. Do they know what happens to caterpillars? Discuss and make sure everyone is clear about caterpillars becoming chrysalises, then becoming butterflies. Emphasise the fact that it's almost as if the caterpillar's life as a caterpillar has to end before it can become a beautiful butterfly. Explain how Jesus died but that meant that He was then able to come back to life and live forever. Jesus is alive today and wants to be our Friend and for us to enjoy life with Him. Jesus promises that if we're His friends we will know He loves us, we'll be happy in life even when things are hard. We can look forward to being with Him forever, i.e. we have a hope and we can know His peace. Then get them to colour in the letters that make up the words LOVE, PEACE, HOPE and JOY and pictures to represent them. Love = Heart; Peace = Dove; Hope = Rainbow; Joy = Happy Smiley Faces. When they've done these, put them up around the display the Starbusters have done today. By the end of this activity you should be able to make a display that looks similar to the example on page 59.

Spend some time praying with them, thanking Jesus that He's alive and that we can be His friends.

Activity 1

Here are some sample badge designs which you could photocopy for the children to draw on and/or colour in.

Peace
Joy
Thank You
JESUS
for
New Life
Hope
Love

Beam Me Up, Swotty

While the children are having their refreshment break, Mary positions herself on the beam spot. The Siren goes off and the space cadets shout 'Beam me up, Swotty!' so that the children sit around the beam spot. As the jingle plays, Swotty appears.

Swotty: Hello and welcome to 'Beam Me Up, Swotty' – sponsored by Comet Cola, the drink that makes you go ... *(Swotty waits for the kids to go 'PING')* The show where we beam up special people from other planets. Well, here we are again. Same time same place but a different person will be beamed up. Let's recap on our fascinating Beamers this week. We had Mary who was the mother to God's Son – Jesus; Simon Peter who had seen Jesus control the fish; Tabitha, the lady that Jesus healed; and yesterday we met Lazarus who was brought back to life by the same man Jesus, when he'd been dead for four days! Private SnugglePuss the Third is beaming us one more person this week and soon we'll get to meet them – I'd really like it to be this Jesus guy. I've been trying to get it out of my director for ages, but he wasn't giving me any clues. Oh well, whoever it is, I can't wait. Let's get on with it ... Starbusters, moonrakers, what are we waiting for? *(kids reply and Mary Magdalene starts moving)* Oh! It doesn't look like it's Jesus, then, folks *(to audience – sounds disappointed)* So hello! My name is Swotty, this is my show. Welcome to 'Beam Me Up, Swotty', sponsored by Comet Cola – *(kids reply)* All we know about you is that you're from Israel, although I've got a slight feeling that you know Jesus, because all of our visitors so far have known Him. Now we're really pleased to have you but I was hoping Jesus would have been beamed up today!

Mary: I'm not sure He could have been actually, from where He is.

Swotty: I hope you're not saying what I think you're saying ... Is He dead?

Mary: Well no ... Well, He was dead but then He wasn't.

Swotty: OK ... *(Confused)* Maybe you'd better tell us a little bit about yourself and how you know Jesus and then we'll get onto whether He's alive!

Mary: Oh, OK. Well, my name's Mary and before I met Jesus I used to spend a lot of time on the streets. I didn't have much money, I wasn't very happy, and I would hear voices in my head telling me bad things. It was a horrible time in my life. I didn't have many friends and my family didn't talk to me. But when I met Jesus He treated me differently. He told the voices to go away and He didn't look at me as if I was nothing, the way other people did.

Swotty: Can you tell us a bit more about that? How did Jesus treat you differently?

Mary: Well He didn't seem to mind where I was from or what I had done, what I looked like or how much money I had. He just loved me for me. So He was kind and gentle and He helped me.

Swotty: So what happened to you after you met Jesus?

Mary: I followed Him everywhere He and His disciples went.

Swotty: Disciples? Who are they?

Mary: They are people who Jesus chose to be with Him. Simon Peter was one of them. Did you say you met him the other day?

Swotty: Ah, yes! Yes we did ... Sorry, where were you?

Mary: Er ... So I followed Jesus everywhere He went and I listened to what He said about God and how we should live. I saw how other people's lives had been changed when He healed them and loved them. Yes, it was amazing. I loved being with Him. But that ended when one of His disciples got Him into trouble with the authorities and they dragged Him through the streets and killed Him.

Swotty: Oh, that's sad ... I want to ask what happens next, which seems a silly question to ask when you've just told me He died but with Jesus you can never tell – He just seems to be able to do anything!

Mary: He can, yes! Well, we took His body and laid it in a tomb. I spent the next couple of days just crying, I couldn't even sleep. I couldn't believe that He was gone. I thought He would be with us forever. I couldn't understand it. Anyway I went down to the tomb very early on the morning of the third day, but when I got there His body was gone! There had been a massive heavy stone covering the entrance, but it had rolled away and the tomb was empty. I thought someone had taken Him – there were lots of people against Jesus. Again I cried. I just sat down and cried. Then the gardener came and asked me why I was crying. He asked me what I was looking for, and then He called me by my name.

Swotty: Did you know Him then?
Mary: I didn't think I did, but then I realised it was Jesus.
Swotty: What! Walking, talking Jesus! Who-had-died Jesus?
Mary: Yes!
Swotty: So He died properly?
Mary: Yes. He was badly beaten, had all His clothes taken away, people shouted at Him and then they nailed Him to a cross and let Him die.
Swotty: Ow! That's got to hurt … So He was dead and lying in tomb with a big rock across it … and then you saw Him alive and well outside the tomb?
Mary: Yes!
Swotty: How do you explain that?
Mary: I can't really. It's a miracle.
Swotty: So you did get to be with Him forever then?!
Mary: Yes.
Swotty: Hang on, though. Why did you say I couldn't beam Him?
Mary: Well, Jesus stayed around for a while with us. But then He went to be with His Father. Although He was leaving He told us all about the Holy Spirit, and He told us that He would never leave us.
Swotty: So He is with you now?
Mary: Yes, He is.
Swotty: That's incredible! So even though I can't beam Him, He's actually with me too?
Mary: Yes, that's right.
Swotty: Amazing! *(Puts his finger in his ear to speak to director)* Will you stop gabbling on! I hear voices too – I wish Jesus would take them away! *(listens again to director)* Oh dear, I think I may have lost my job! Anyway, I'm afraid we really do need to finish there, Mary. Thanks to my audience – as ever you've been great. And thank you to my last Beamer of the week, Mary Magdalene, another Mary, who has been telling us about how Jesus from Israel around AD 30, Planet Earth, died, then came back to life and is still alive today! I'm going to find out more about this Jesus as I'll have a bit of spare time while I'm collecting the dole! Anyway, thanks, Mary. Let's give her a big round of applause to beam her back to Earth.

(As they clap Mary waves but slowly begins to freeze. The jingle plays, Swotty waves goodbye and goes off. Do a couple of Emergency Smergencies during which Mary disappears.)

DAY 5

M:MM Homequest

Well it's our last Homequest today! We hope you've enjoyed learning all about the Miracle Maker, Jesus. It's been great having the Topz Gang help us too. If you'd like to find out more about them and also find out more about Jesus, then you could try getting your hands on a copy of *Topz*, it's great fun. Well, I guess it's time to meet our last Topz Gang members. So here's Danny and Paul!

*Hey, boys and girls! Nice to meet you all. I'm Danny and I love being in the Topz Gang! I'm a bit of a **Star Wars** fan. I've seen all the films at least three times, the special effects are so cool. I also love football. I'm in the school team and I've even managed to score a few goals.*

And I'm Paul – the Gang's computer wizard! I've programmed today's miracle into my computer, and it's jumbled the words all up. See if you can unjumble it.

ueJss asw radeis rofm het adde nad si valie adtoy!

It's so cool knowing Jesus, He really is alive. He's my best Friend and helps me all the time. In fact there's a bit in the Bible which we're going to try and learn now where Jesus promises never to leave us. Here it is. See if you can learn it off by heart.

Jesus said: 'I am with you always, to the very end of the age.'

*Even when **Mission: Miracle Maker** is over you can still carry on getting to know Jesus because He's everywhere. We can pray to Him anytime. I hope you enjoy getting to know Jesus. Well, we've nearly finished but first see if you can join Jesus back up with His disciples – they've got separated in the maze.*

Oh no – I'm afraid there's just enough space for one last joke from Benny, before we say goodbye …

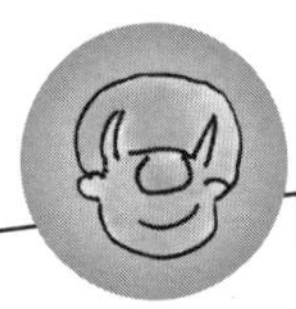

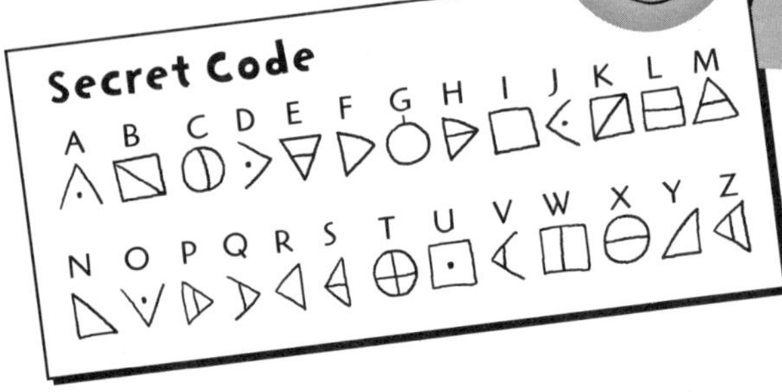

Benny's Joke

If you drop a white hat into the Red Sea, what does it become?

*OK! I'm afraid it's time to say goodbye to you all. It's been great to be a part of **Mission: Miracle Maker**. Bye! See you all again in Topz!*